I Blame The Tornado

N.S. Burdette

I Blame The Tornado

I struggle to breathe my lungs caving in.
The loud fit of nature, the horrible wind.
Afraid to close my eyes ever brief.
No matter how much I crave the relief.
I sit alone, shed silent tears
Praying the torture doesn't last for years
I cant explain, the emotions that hit
so I struggle alone, just as I sit
would a touch or hug help me cope
is it just the empathy I need or hope
I pray each night my mind can clear
the trembling dread my body holds near
alone is how this battle will rage
before my life can turn the last page

Written By
N.S. Burdette

I Blame The Tornado

No one prepares you for life in its entirety, I mean your parents love and provide the basics but predicting the future just doesn't happen. Don't misunderstand me I know my parents love me and I would take a bullet for my kids because I love them so much but everyday life just happens. You get an aha moment from time to time and will ask yourself a billion times "what if?". I have been there and if you can't relate you are in denial.

Every step you take, every decision you make impacts your direction and outcome. The journey is just part of this adventure, it's the moments you capture each day that make up your story.

I have said all that to move on to this....

I grew up in a small rural community where when the streetlight came on (we only had one) you had better be in your own yard. If you heard the bell ring, food was on the table (seriously, we had a bell just a hair smaller than the liberty bell mounted by our back door that mom would ring to alert us all that dinner was on the table). The neighbor kids had a whistle their dad would blow and that was their call (not going to lie I mimicked it on occasion to make them run home just for fun). We had a small grocery store and 2 gas pumps (we were living large for sure). Everyone knew who you belonged too and didn't hesitate to bust you for questionable behavior (not speaking from experience in any way). Most families were large and we were no exception.

My parents raised 8 children (they had 9 children total but that's a story for another time). I repeated moms rhyme anytime anyone asked who my brothers and sisters were......
 Pammie, Tammie, Vickie, Nicky, Ricky, Jimmy, Johnny, Ann, Norma Sue (with that many of us how else do you remember them all, that's me at the end). In no particular order as I was actual the 6th child born in this brood. It was my sister Vickie who gracefully pointed out that our parents were breeders not readers (shudder).

We camped in the summers and survived horrible winters without frostbite while skating on Strueblers pond or sledding at the Yorkville hill (monster snow covered hill before the fated subdivisions took over). We attended the very small Methodist church that my parents were married in (I too would go on to marry my best friend in that very church).
Life was simple, it was the 70's and the 80's after all. We didn't get text, Twitter or snap chat and our only dial phone (you read that right, dial phone) was attached to the kitchen wall with a 25 foot cord for privacy (I had many chats in the laundry room growing up). Ducking the cord could have been an Olympic sport in our house no question.

My parents were great role models, they loved one another dearly and never took life too seriously (did I mention they raised 8 kids). I think I was 9 when I realized my mothers name was in fact NOT Jeezuschristnancy. My father took everything in stride and my mother loved to keep him on his toes.
Mom and dad filled our days with stories or antics that kept life growing up in that little town exciting. They showed us what

unconditional love and commitment with a splash of crazy was and most of us kept that with us in our adult lives.

Examples of crazy include……….. Mom paying neighbor kids to pop up the parquet wood flooring before my dad got home from work because she wanted carpeting (this was definitely something I stored in my brain for later in life). We had 3 or 4 neighbor kids crawling around the living room floor with screw drivers, kitchen knives and hammers popping up tile after tile. Mom paid us all in dimes and we were happy to help cause the destruction. When dad arrived home from work and saw the carnage he just said "you are still not getting carpet" (challenge accepted).

The following day my mother, in true Banksy form, used purple spray paint to add the finishing touches (something to the affect of "bare with me, my husband is a cheap s.o.b. and won't buy me carpeting"). This glowing statement was large enough to cover the floor but you had to walk and read as you came in the front door. When dad got home there was no way he would miss this plea but he just smiled and shook his head. We waited a whole year to get carpet but we eventually covered the artwork on the floor. Poor visitors had nothing to read once the carpet went in.

My mom was always eager to keep life interesting.

My father had to attend a nice dinner for work and everyone attending was dressed up. Mom was comfortable in her pants but would pretty up for dad. Mom was dressed up in a very nice dress and dad in jacket and tie and off they went. While seated at the table mom noticed the other wives were well endowed and the pleats on their blouses were puckered, not to be out done mom excused herself to use the restroom. When she returned to the table she too had the puckered pleats in her blouse (have I mentioned my dad is a saint?). As the evening progressed the wives got more animated. At one point a glass of wine was tipped over and mom without hesitation reached into her bra and started pulling out toilet tissue to soak up the spill. Mom just told the other wives "don't worry, I got this". My dad just rolls his eyes and laughs whenever we talk about this, that folks is unconditional love!

On another occasion we were at a picnic for dads work surrounded by other families. The kids played while the adults socialized. Mom was raised to be genuine so when she was asked how she can feed 8 kids she didn't hesitate with her response. My mom simply looked the other mothers over and stated "it's simple, I line the children up, each holding a bun. I tie a hotdog up with a string and pull, the child that bites first gets the hotdog". My dad made a nice wage and it was enough that mom never had to work. Because the woman was so arrogant mom felt her response was warranted. Safe to say if you met my mom, you remembered my mom (same applies to this day)!

Our lives were made up of so many of these stories that we all knew to take life as it came and roll with the punches. Our home was not very big but there always seemed to be room for the extra kid who occasionally needed a place to stay. Mom became the mom to a few non genetically linked kids but never once treated anybody with indifference. She just made room and all the same rules applied.

My father was a strong believer in home cooking, so our meals were usually a family recipe made with dads own hands. Mom was domestically challenged and had a limited number of menu options but whatever it was, it was always ready at dinner time (I recall a rice incident that involved more pans than our kitchen held- definitely an I Love Lucy moment if you follow me) and yes the bell was rung.
Don't for a minute think mom was not fierce, she stood just over 5 feet tall but she could hold her own (that is where I get my spunk for sure).

Did I mention at the ripe old age of 5 I quit kindergarten?

Mom picked me up when I demanded the school call her. Youngest drop out in the history of Serena grade school (they wouldn't teach me to read, what's a girl to do?). My mother made me stand and face my dad when he got home from work and explain what I had done. Dad looked at me and asked "what's the matter with my fairy princess" Mom stood her ground and said "tell your father why your not in school" I explained to dad that they were "all dumb and wouldn't teach me to read so I quit"! There was no way I was going back and no one could make me………

Well, I returned the following year as a 2nd time kindergartner (proud moment for sure).

As a large family we were close and never without supervision. We had rules and chore lists we had to follow but with 8 of us (and the occasional extra kids) it wasn't a nightmare. We were all pretty close in age but enough of a gap to go different directions often.

Being the youngest girl had its advantages, rules weakened by the time I could break them. I was a daddy's girl through and through (his fairy princess) but prided myself on being a tomboy.

That was, until I figured out I liked boys more.

I never had an interest in being anyone's girlfriend, I liked my freedom and just wasn't ready to be kissed. By the time I hit high school I started seeing boys in a different light. I didn't date, party or sneak out, I just admired from afar. Until I met a beautiful boy (my dad always says "boys are not beautiful, they are handsome") but this boy was beautiful. His eyes were so green and his skin was so golden brown I was hooked from the first moment I saw him.
 I was 15 and it was summertime and I couldn't tear my eyes away from his smile. Our small little town hosted softball games which was the most activity any of us ever saw. It was either softball at the park or soda at the small grocery store for entertainment.

Weeks passed by and I looked forward to the one day a week I could just watch him play softball. He would casually speak to me and he joked a bit, we became friends and it was nice. It was when I got the call that he wanted to take me to the movies that everything changed. I thought I was dreaming and prayed nobody would wake me.

Now my mom had a dating rule (must be 16 to date) but I was the 4th daughter and I was just 3 months shy of the big one six so with fingers crossed I asked.
After a confirmation from my older brother Nick that the man asking me out was a nice guy I was given the green light to go on my very first date.
Good lord in heaven was I nervous.

The moment my date arrived to pick me up, I was nearly running from the house. Not fast enough, as my mom stepped onto the porch to get a visual of my suitor. As she made eye contact with this handsome creature she simply held up her pinky finger and waved it in the air. Some of you may see where this is going, yep, I was mortified. It's when he asked what she was doing my mom replied for me with "you don't deserve the best" (kill me now). It was then that I saw the most heart stopping smile on his face (dear god I am in love). This gorgeous man was amused by my mother and her crazy antics and not offended, he was a keeper!

Jump ahead a few years ….

Here I was, being walked down the aisle by my father in a small country church my parents walked down 25 years earlier. I was marrying my best friend and he just so happened to be the beautiful boy I had my very first date with. Yup you heard me right, I married my first real boyfriend, my very first date and the only boy who ever really kissed me. The stars aligned and I was going to live the fairy tale, right?

The first years of marriage were a test no question. We fought, we made up, we fought some more. So many times we were broken and then healed. We got through everything together. We struggled and grew stronger because of it.
We brought 3 amazing children (Emory, Casie & Philip) into the world and survived our battle wounds. We worked hard to raise wonderful adults and create a home for them. We saw these amazing kids through tough times and small victories. We used lots of parenting skills we never realized we had, to make them amazing people.

Years flew by and college tuition came upon us faster than we were ready for.
Together we made it work and 2 of our 3 children graduated from 4 year colleges. Our daughter (Casie) chose another path and gave us our first 2 grandsons (6 years later our youngest son Philip provided us with our 3rd grandson).

Our hearts were full.

Our children had all flown the nest and now it was just us (oh god, it's just us!).

Bob and I thought long and hard on where our future should lead us. Our children were off making their way in the world and we were empty nesters. Bob had retired after 32 years with the State of Illinois and we were ready for our next chapter. We decided we needed to move south and spend time enjoying the life we made. We would spend the next year searching for our forever home in the south.

In April of 2016 we found our dream home with the help of my youngest brother Rick. This home was nestled on top a mountain overlooking another mountain with amazing views. It was built by a doctor as a vacation home but it was now my "retirement" sanctuary. It had room for family and friends to visit and close to family I hadn't really spent time with in over 30 years (my parents retired to this beautiful southern town years earlier). Life was headed in the fairy tale direction and I was living it with that beautiful boy I met 35 years prior. It took a few months to get surveys, inspections and contracts drawn up but in October of 2016 we closed on our dream home.

We listed our home in Illinois and decided when it sold we would make the move.
I was having a hard time with this, we raised all 3 of our children in this home. We lived in the same home for 27 years. How do we let someone else create memories in OUR home?
Although I struggled with this decision, our dream home awaited us.
Bob would make trips getting things ready in our new home so when we moved it would be a breeze (that was the plan and it sounded like a good one).
I remained working at the same place I had been for 20 years, a job I loved.
So for the next few months Bob would drive down to our new home and work on changes we needed to make and take boxes that were making the move. On a few occasions I was able to make the trip with him and help get things in order. Since our new home was twice the size I found myself picking up furniture

often so we could fill it. Bob never questioned why no matter how much he moved, he would come home to see more stuff to be moved in the garage. We had plenty of time and plenty of trips to make south, Bob had this (that was my pep talk every time we loaded our enclosed trailer with each trip).

We decided to spend New Years Eve in our mountain home so we could move some furniture in (I think Bob was secretly planning an intervention on my furniture shopping). When we arrived at 1am we had no water. Surely it wasn't cold enough to freeze and I know the water was turned on. Bob decided to investigate under the house (maybe we had bigger issues with this house than we initially thought). As soon as he crawled under the house the power went out (I kid you not, I had visions of Tom Hanks in Money Pit running through my head). I remember thinking what evil game is this? I was exhausted (it was a 9 hour drive after working 9 hours), cold and getting annoyed. We decided (as in me) to just get a nap and attack this with fresh eyes. By 7am the power company was knocking on the door to help with the power issue (I forgot I called them to report the outage). Long story short power was back on but no luck on the water.
This was spinning into an adventure of large per portion.

I would love to say we figured out the water situation and enjoyed the new year in peace but that would be a lie. Since our water runs along our 1 mile driveway before it gets to the house (the meter is a mile from the house-gahhhh). Several long walks looking for any puddles were fruitless until mid day when we realized there was a connection we didn't check in the "holler" (I cannot make this up, the water line comes up from the holler).

Quick inspection of this connection and yup repairs were in order. No signs of water buildup so it couldn't be that bad, right? Well one call to the water company revealed 200,000 gallons of missing water! You have got to be kidding me? It appears the caves in the mountain would absorb the water so no signs would show above ground (good to know).

Welcoming 2017 was looking like a challenge, but we were ready to face these new adventures together, bring it!

Be careful what you wish for comes to mind a lot these days……

February 28th 2017 started like any other work day. Bob was in Arkansas working on a bathroom remodel preparing to come to Illinois in the next couple days. I decided I would hit the grocery store on the way home from work to gather some baking supplies (my work family was in brownie withdrawal due to my lack of attention). My plan was to get home and fire up the oven and start a large batch of brownies. I noticed the sky looking cloudy but nothing out of the ordinary for February in Illinois.
I made it home from the store and noticed the power flicker but not go out so I decided to put my supplies away and change into my baking attire. I looked out the kitchen window and saw my neighbor gathering up his child's yard playsets and bikes and moving them close to his house. I headed down the hallway to get changed still not concerned with the weather. I was stopped short of my bedroom when the power went out. As soon as the house went black I heard the loudest sound I have ever heard in my life. The noise went on for what seemed like hours (in reality it was just minutes but I am a woman so you know). I felt fear all

the way to my bones and was just frozen in place.

I had no idea what was happening but realized something was wrong when I started getting soaked, my glasses and hair were getting rained on! I think my brain was trying to tell my legs to do something but my body was not having it.
It was too dark to see anything even though it wasn't even 4:30 in the afternoon. I remember at one point trying to get out of the house but couldn't open the patio doors (good thing because I was apparently in a tornado). I ran back to the hall for no reason as the clouds cleared and saw that the 200 year old oak tree (12.5 feet around and 90 feet tall) had slammed through our house right in front of where I was standing. The tree snapped a bedroom door in half and sealed off 2 of the bedrooms, one of which I was going into. Before you ask, no I didn't soil my shorts, I had no comprehension of what happened. I don't remember being on the phone when it hit and I don't remember texting or calling anyone but I apparently did (to those people I have to apologize for the crazy).
I remember my boys (Emory ran the few blocks to my house barefoot & Philip who drove over trees) and my brother Nick coming to save me but not much else.

They say your body has a way of protecting you and for that I am grateful. I think had I been aware of what was happening the outcome could have been very different (not in a good way). Emory climbed through the doorway where the tree had fallen and grabbed some clothes for me out of the closet. Once I made it out the door I saw there were neighbors in my yard with a police officer. The neighbor was not aware that I was home so they didn't know anyone was inside. I assured them I was not harmed, my boys and brother were here so I would be fine.

I was not even remotely fine so Philip packed me up and took me to his house. The storm continued to rage even after the tornado and hale was pounding the windows causing me to lose my shit. Katie (Philips wife) was working at the hospital when it hit so she was fine but worried about me. When she finally made it home she had a toothbrush and a few other things I would need for the next couple days. Emory and his wife Keri were ok and their house like Philips was spared. It was a relief to know my children were safe (the storm missed my daughters town). Katie's father waited hours at the only restaurant open to get us food but there was just no way I could eat anything.

Thankfully I got through the meltdown but now I was homeless and Bob was not here.

I was apparently on the phone with my mother in Arkansas when it hit so she made frantic calls for help to my brother and husband. Bob drove through the night and made it to me before the sun came up.
For days I could not sleep, afraid I would realize I was in the bedroom changing and didn't make it out. Just another way your brain works when it doesn't. I cannot even put it into words but trust me when I say that is some scary shit!

Pause here for my mental breakdown……

The fear that keeps me from closing my eyes,
The sounds before I met my demise.

Had I known why I felt so uneasy,
Would I have done any part of the day differently?

It haunts me when I try to escape,
These moments, the noise I have grown to hate.

If I sleep will my body discover the truth,
That I didn't make it all the way through.

Why cant my emotions release the tear,
Close my eyes and get over this fear.

Letting go of these haunting visions,
My future plans left unwritten.

A moment in time that continues to play,
Over and over every single day.

Will it get any better with time,
Or will my normal require lots of wine?

Jump ahead to the clean up……

Day one after the tornado and the news crews from Chicago set up right in front of our house. Cameras were everywhere and reporters were constantly invading our grief. We couldn't get away from them and photos of our home made every station as well as newspaper. I was actually reported to be "the elderly woman who sought refuge in the bathroom". Now I never spoke to any reporter but I guess I did feel elderly after a few days of cleaning up debris (roll with the punches).

We spent days saving what we could, cleaning up debris. The insurance company couldn't assess the damage until we had the tree removed. How the hell do we get a 27,000 pound tree removed from our house?
Friends, family and strangers came in groups to help. Churches delivered soup and water to us as we worked on picking up the pieces. We found a tree removal company who spent hours cutting and pulling this oak monster off our house. 11 dump trucks and 2 logging trucks later the tree was gone.
It took days to realize how bad it actually was (the house had to come down, nothing could be saved).
We were fortunate enough to be offered a place to stay (Philips in laws were headed to Florida for a few months so they gave us their home to rest our heads) while we saved, packed and loaded what was left of our lives.
I was able to give notice and work a few weeks before leaving my job. Saying goodbye to everyone and leaving was hard but we knew we had a place to go.
We gave the property to a construction company in exchange for tearing down the house (I couldn't watch those memories being loaded into a dumpster and hauled away) and cleaning up the property.

 Now we had no choice but to move to our mountain home and begin our next chapter.

I call the next chapters my adventure to crazy and yes, I blame the tornado.
Not a day goes by that doesn't in some way remind me to roll with the punches. Never take life too seriously and just enjoy the

ride (I think that's a Yahtzee in the life hack quotes).

First example of my new crazy……

The home we purchased in Arkansas was once hit by a tree (I did not know this).
So follow me here, not only was our house in Illinois a welcome mat for the arbor variety but our new piece of paradise kissed the bark too.
Just fabulous!

All I could think about was the movie, The World According to Garp (when the plane flew into the house they wanted to buy) I mean what are the odds of it happening again, right?

We loaded up a U-Haul with what we could save and headed south, 9 hours south to be exact. We unloaded the truck and began putting our lives back together, one tote at a time. And believe you me panic packed totes are much less productive when unpacking than new adventure excited totes.

Our next chapter was beginning whether we were ready for it or not.
The moment I pulled up to our gate I was struck with panic. This was not a vacation, there was no going home again, this was home now.
We unloaded the trailer and slowly began sorting through all the totes and boxes filling the garage with anything that could wait. Settling in would be slow going but we have the rest of our lives to get through it all.

Once we got somewhat organized we realized we needed to create more storage and a work space for Bob.

We decided we needed to add a barn to our Ozark spread. Bob deserved a space, he worked hard to retire and needed a place for his future projects (ok my projects…..but whatever). We actually found one online described as an erector set for adults. Bob and I could handle this. We tackled remodels and rebuilds and survived a tornado, this should be gravy, right?

First lesson, NEVER buy something this large without, seeing, touching or licking it in person.

We waited for our blue prints to arrive, the anticipation was insane. When they finally arrived we tore the package open like it was Christmas morning. Little did we know we would abruptly lose that enthusiasm like Ralphy opening pink bunny Jammie's (Christmas story reference, gonna be a few of those).
The blue prints looked like a first grade art project.
The measurements were best guesses and the customer service was a tin can and a string.
Lord help me.
We scheduled the delivery truck which turned out to be a semi and waited. We had to make arrangements with the local home center to borrow a large fork truck (they don't tell you all the good parts when you order these things). Then we had to unload the crates in the neighboring field because "off the grid" is not delivery truck friendly.
Once the crates were on the ground and the truck drove away we were the proud owners of a 30 x 40 steel building (ok, proud

owners of a few crates of steel parts).

As overwhelming as the field o crates was, we still couldn't wait to get this thing up. This building was larger than we initially thought but we have mad skills, seriously we got this, right?

Well, do you have any idea how tall 23 feet is?
I mean looking from the ground up. Do you have any idea what steel weighs when assembling said building?
From sun up to sun down we were sorting and counting parts of this "adult erector set". You would think it was the Eiffel Tower in a crate when pulling this stuff out. We had just a few days to report any issues (seriously who would want to go through pages upon pages of parts, we had a building to put up). Summer was fast approaching and we had a building to erect.

By the time we received missing parts, then corrected parts it was the height of summer (ok maybe not height of summer but April in the Ozarks feels like the surface of the sun to this Yankee).
Do you have any idea how hot the sun gets or how hot metal gets sitting in said sun?
Let me just say that by the time we set everything out and started putting it together I had to look around for the film crew. What started out as a bonding project for Bob's new workshop turned into a long season of "forged in fire". Moving 100lb. molten hot steel beams without oven mits was a challenge to say the least. We worked long days with many hours in direct sunlight. We reached a point where we needed to raise the 3 framed sections that everything would bolt to. These end wall and center section weighed in excess of 900 lbs so walking them up to bolt to the

slab was not going to happen. We calculated a lot of angles but decided with one telephone pole, lots of chain and 2 John Deere tractors we could raise them ourselves. I should have set up a camera to capture this redneck, backwoods barn raising dance of death but I was too concerned with avoiding the ER. As we hooked the chains to the frame, ran them up over the pole that we had braced with angle iron we hooked the chain to the winch attached to one tractor. As we are winching the tractor begins to slide (time to regroup). Bob fires up tractor 2 and parks it next to tractor 1 and fires up the winch. This is why I married this man (ok, maybe that is stretching it), he can do anything! The frame started to stand and only took a little manuvering and we had the makings of a barn starting. At one point we needed to use bigger equipment to get the upper roof beams installed. Now Bob is not good with heights but having worked 20 years in a warehouse I have the equipment experience which, by process of elimination, placed Bob in the basket.

At this point I notice that we should have cleared some trees before we began this project but of course we did not think ahead.

Bob climbed into the basket on the skylift and I got behind the wheel. Things appeared to be running smoothly, I was getting a feel for the controls and I was lifting and extending the basket while Bob bolted roof supports. God we are an amazing team! Spoke too soon.....

As Bob is bolting the outer wall horizontal beams he signals me to lift him up. Well, I was sitting in direct sunlight and zoning out so I missed the first request. Its when Bob yells to get my attention that I jump and start extending the basket into a tree. Realizing my mistake I jerk the basket and start raising the boom causing

Bob to lose his footing.
If Bob was not afaid of heights before he sure as shit was now! Bob screams for me to stop at which point I vacate the truck leaving him stranded in the air and in a tree (not my finest moment).
Bob looks down at me and calmly tells me to get him down and we would break for a bit. I eventually get Bob down and out of the tree, grateful it was just bark burn and not broken bones. Several long hot months later we were looking at the mother of all barns. Ahhhhh, proud moment right there.

Pause for life events here....

Relationships can and do fail. Marriages can and do fall apart. If 2 people part ways most of the time it is for the best in the long run. If during said relationship you were blessed with a child or children, they are not part of that failure. Children do not have the option to chose their parents but I am certain that if they could chose they would pick a loving, caring take a bullet for you kind of parent.

That being said....

If you father a child or children and refuse to support said child or children you are Not a parent. If you brag about newly obtained "extras" while your children do without. You are Not a parent. Being able to procreate does not make you a parent, it makes you a donor. If you are a donor who fails to provide for your child or children you are (I will simplify this) A PIECE OF GARBAGE! There is no "do over" when raising a child or children and when you fail them, that makes you a FAILURE!

So if you are a donor piece of garbage failure and this offends you.....too bad!
If you are unsure please read this again!!!

More words that are stuck in my head.......

> My heart breaks a little bit each day,
> A fathers love just walked away.
>
> The joys and laughter I get to see,
> Is one he will never share with me.
>
> The children's lives he forgot all about,
> Because he would rather live without.
>
> It is only him who will ultimately suffer,
> He cant take any more from another.
>
> I will love them enough for us both,
> And protect for life my solemn oath.
>
> My boys are my life to love completely,
> A fathers love they will no longer see.
>
> The selfish choices of those in this world,
> Impact the future of so many souls.
>
> My boys will be strong and loved forever,
> Because I am a strong, fierce single mother.

Fast forward to May 2017..........

We get the news are daughter and grandsons are coming down to live with us. We will get 24/7 with these 2 little guys!
Not going to lie I can't wait to get my hands on these 2. Empty nesting isn't all it's cracked up to be. I need baby snuggles to fill my days since I am among the unemployed.
We had barely unloaded all the chaos from the urgent move (thanks to mothers natures wrath) and we were bringing another household down.
We hooked up the trailer and headed back to Illinois to load up our daughter Casie and our grandsons.
Time for another chapter and a fresh start for these three.
Life is full of twists and turns but I am a believer in the "everything happens for a reason" adage. There was a higher purpose for this chapter and we were all ready.

A full truck and trailer loaded with precious cargo and we were headed south again.
Now we just had to figure out where we would put everything……
We had the room but space was getting tight.
Once we all arrived at the paradise on the mountain we had to get these newbies settled. We had a lot of new boxes and furniture to unload and dont even get me started on the toys!

Fortunately we had a decent sized enclosed trailer that would help the storage struggle (until your grandson NEEDS his stuffed cow which is apparently in a box marked miscellaneous).
Declan was absolutely adament that he get his cow out of the trailer.
You can't tell a sad faced little boy to wait until you can organize

to find a beloved stuffed cow.
We now have the urgent task of locating a stuffed cow in walls of "miscellaneous" boxes.
The unloading and searching was a high priority.
 As with anything new and interesting the boys are going to be elbows in.
Now unloading wasn't a big deal, at this point if it was an Olympic sport we would score a gold.
As we begin, we see we need to remove the spare tire from the trailer (follow me here it starts to get good).
We take the tire out and the boxes begin to come out and get opened in search of the evasive cow. Commotion to the left causes us to exit the trailer just in time to see the spare tire being rolled down the hill and toward the deep wooded hollar. Declan laughing hysterically because he got it to roll all by himself. Bob frantically sprinting toward the tire trying feverishly to catch it but of course the tire disappeared before he could reach it.
A couple of things running through my mind. Declan figured out how to lift, stand and roll the brand new spare tire (pretty proud of his thought process and implementation skills). Bob hasn't had to run that fast in years so the forced cardio was certainly a plus, right?
But now someone had to retrieve the tire from the sketchy hollar that no one has ventured into in what I am guessing decades.
I of course screamed "not it" because I apparently never grew up and thought that was going to exempt me from this process.
Bob simply looked at me, shook his head and started walking into the woods.
Days like this make me believe I married a man like my father.

Long story short the tire came out unscathed and Bob made it band aide free but the big win was one located stuffed cow.
Time to get these kids settled into their new home.
I can tell you after raising our children it will be an adventure having little ones around 24/7. I may need therapy in the process but we got this.
It is amazing how you can picture sunshine and rainbows in your head and then reality bitch slaps you into the here and now with the blink of an eye.
Living off the grid is amazing, well unless you're 5 and 7 apparently because then it becomes the hell that will ruin their lives (almost a direct quote).
I never had to move from my home while growing up, I never left lifelong friends behind so trying to understand the issues we would face was tough. Staying busy was the plan and keeping the boys entertained until school started was key. Once school started they would have structure, new friends and activities.
Just 3 months to wait, oh god 3 months!

We need a game plan, I mean call in favors, line up the troupes. This will be the longest summer vacation of my life!

Bob and I decided that maybe creating a new structure would help……………

We decided as a family that Thursday nights would be movie night. We have a vast library of dvd's to watch so it was kids choice. Blankets, popcorn and lots of cuddles once the sun set and it was movie time.
The dog had other plans as he climbed the couch to get a better

view outside. Lots of whimpering and staring was cause for concern.

We were pretty new to this remote living and had no idea what creatures were outside visiting.

Upon close inspection into the dark yard (no streetlights or even moon light to help) I was confronted with the biggest brown eyes attached to a giant head -yikes (a cow had entered the yard from the neighboring farm and decided to enjoy movie night).

The dog decides at this point to cease all movement and go silent.

I take this moment to run to the front door and look out to see what was going on. Pitch black night was of no help. I grabbed the emergency light (for power outages or creepy yard invaders) and shine it into the yard.

There in the yard were about 20 sets of eyes glowing back at me. We had a bovine yard party going on and of course they were dropping yard bombs everywhere.

Side note……

Did you know that cows poop when they run?
Did you know that 20 cows pooping as they run causes an unholy mess that stays with you for days?

Yeah me neither.

Picture if you will 2 children and 2 adults screaming and shooing cows down the driveway in the dark of night while trying to avoid

getting splattered with natures paintballs.
Not a moment I want to relive any time soon.

Summer was starting out full of adventurous fun. This was just a taste of what "off the grid" had to offer.

Do you have any idea what summer in the Ozarks mountains is like?
The tiny little critters that climb into very inconvenient places and set up camp.
I have never in my life had to check anyone but my dog for ticks!

Until my first summer in my dream home.

I have the wonderful web to guide me so I don't look too uneducated to any locals (because saving face and avoiding embarrassment certainly supersedes asking skilled professionals for help).

Just so you all know putting oil on a tick DOES NOT get that sucker to retreat, it only makes it harder to grab (they breathe out their butt and you suffocate them with oil my aunt fanny).

These ticks are hybrids and once they have you for dinner you are claiming them as dependents on your 1040, true story.

Chiggers are another critter that will ruin your day. These bastards should be enlisted in our armed forces with their stealth like appearance. Seriously, you have no idea they have even invaded until it's too late (and by too late I mean tore your flesh off scratching and digging like your mining for gold). I now understand why everyone wears pants in the summer down here while working in the fields.

Lesson learned!

The Ozarks also offer up a multitude of flying creatures from hell. Did you know there are red wasps the size of a go pro camera. Seriously these things take flight like the monkeys in the wizard of oz (the original Oz not the CGI version). They latch on to everything and make it their home.
Picture if you will my kitchen broom handle swinging and slapping the flying spawn of Satan like I was training in martial arts (ninja skills are learned by using this method).
I worked for weeks clearing these squatters off my front porch (I mean really how would I collect rent).
I couldn't wait to put rocking chairs and the retirement scene out there and these guys were cramping my HGTV vibe.

Once I eradicated every sign of the Red Devils my broom (aka the saber of death) was placed back into service as it was designed (coat hook until someone spills something).
My porch became a sanctuary of rocking bliss where blue tailed lizards could be observed and birds could be fed (remember this tidbit of information for a future rant).

Back to the porch and my happy place......

Since it was so serene and peaceful on the newly claimed porch I

would sit and watch my grandsons at play.
The dog (Dyme Bag- he came to us with that name don't judge) at my feet watching natures beauty.
Life was good, until dark when the gauntlet was thrown down.

I should start with Dyme being a small spoiled black Shih Tzu who only walks when he wants to.
So when night came and it was last call for his personal business I let him out to get rid of his inner most thoughts.
He came to the door and waited patiently for his, (I didn't go in the house) treat and was ready to retreat upstairs.

Did I mention spoiled?

He sleeps all cuddled up in bed with us and doesn't think twice about where he will stay (with his I own the bed and you better recognize attitude). This boy is so spoiled he can't be bothered to climb the 11 stairs to rest his head. He will stand at the base of the stairs and stare at you until you pick him up and carry him (I mean, I tried to play hardball with him but the guilt he can inflict requires weeks of therapy, so I caved).

So, on this evening I bent down and scooped up cute little Dyme Bag and tucked him in like a receiver at the Super Bowl for the trek up the stairs.
 It was just then a stabbing pain pierced my right rib cage where Dyme was tucked!
Are you freaking kidding me what the hell was that and where did the dirty prison shank that just pierced my lung come from?
I needed light and I was certain stitches for the carnage I would

uncover.

I looked the dog over and there was nothing!

I was certain I was headed for the pearly gates. I looked around the floor for any knives, shanks, needles or the little native doll from trilogy of terror because something wanted me dead.

Slight movement caught my attention on the floor.

Mother Mary and Joseph it was a flying red devil sauntering across the floor with a "take that bitch" smirk (really I saw this demon smirk at me). I did the only thing I could think to do in that moment, I grabbed a slipper and put in on my foot (Bob's rant to put slippers on my feet playing over in my head) and stomped that bastard into sidewalk art. There was literally nothing left that a Lysol wipe couldn't handle.

When I finally made my way upstairs with Dyme in tow (not tucked in the football hold but more like stinky shoes at arms length) to get to a mirror and meds. The welt and burning the evil bastard left me with was insane.

I mean I gave birth to a 10 pound baby with no medication (Philip Andrew you are welcome) and this made that seem aspirin worthy.

Dear lord in heaven how can you give this much power to a wasp?

Well, it took 4 days for the pain to go away and 9 days for the swelling to go down.

Never piss off gods creatures because they bring the wrath of Satan when they come at you.

Again, lesson learned.

This move to our dream home was challenging and proving it

more every day.
I mean I really do love the Ozarks (even with the newly discovered creatures) and our new home. The scenery and the lifestyle is just what we needed......but it poses more challenges than that of the insect variety.

Like do you realize there is no trash pick up off the grid?
Seriously, nobody comes and picks up your garbage at all.
You are left to your own devices when it comes to your unwanted trash.
Then there are the critters, not just the cows that occasionally visit but like serious critters. The ugliest most disturbing critters I've only ever seen in cartoons growing up.
I am in no way a city girl , I mean I fished, camped Gigged a frog or two and even caught crawfish but this right here is on a whole different level.

So back to the trash pick up thing (I get sidetracked easily).

Since we have to "run to the dump" to dispose of our weekly trash you have to be smart on bagging it and placing it in cans (reference critter description above). So I was looking in the refrigerator to see what I could "safely" dispose of and found an aging fruit tray that had to go. Knowing there was no way I could bag this "safely" I thought I could toss it into the "holler" for the critters and birds to feast on (keeping them a safe distance from our house).
Well, as I was tossing the fruit, the container slipped out of my hands and into the very tall timberesk (I know this isn't a word but go with it) area.

Now I stood there, contemplating walking away (not like me to litter but I was not looking forward to meeting any new national geographic monsters) and I just couldn't walk away.

I assessed the area only to notice the empty tray lodged behind the most terrifying rose bush (prehistoric tree is a better description). I swear to you I felt my heart in my throat. My decision to retrieve it didn't change but I started questioning my sanity.

My thought was to carefully move the branch (carefully was so not going to happen) and reach down to grab the tray. As I moved the branch I slipped causing the branch the snap back into the back of my hand (yup I was certain the hand of satan just shredded my flesh). Realizing the pain I was in I had to pull my hand out fast (and didn't have time to analyze the situation) and the branch shot back and smacked me in the stomach.

Now you cannot make this stuff up, I immediately looked around for witnesses (not for miles, I know). I half expected Bob to be standing behind me laughing his butt off at the comedic episode I was starring in. Fortunately I was alone in my misery.

Once I retrieved the tray and ran to the house to evaluate the number of band aids this would require I realized I was covered in thorns from the rose tree (seriously it had bark).

I began to remove each one only to see I had burrs in my hair! How did it fling burrs in my hair?

Was this a Mother Nature scolding for contemplating the litter aspect?

 About an hour into my surgical residency I decided, its Bob's job to clean out the fridge and manage the trash.

My work here is done!

The summer days rolled by quickly and we were just weeks away from the start of a new school year. The back deck was a nice retreat from the sun with amazing views of the mountain. The boys played music and relaxed on the deck while playing. Watching the cute little blue tailed lizards scurry around. Nature and its wonders right in our back yard. We had birds that made our sanctuary their home. So many different birds came up to feed but none as determined as the cute little humming birds.

These amazing tiny creatures (which we initially thought were large bees because they flew by so fast you only heard them, never seeing them) would dive bomb you if the feeders were empty. I learned early on to keep these things fed. We had a cardinal that would follow you to any room and peck non stop on the window until you put food out. This "crazy bird" would follow you upstairs, to the bathroom, even around to the front of the house. So full feeders was mandatory for our peace and sanity. The boys got to the point they would check the feeders before opening the doors.

So back to the humming birds.....

We had family over visiting and the deck seemed to be the place to gather.
Now I know the tiny birds were out there but they were fed so we were going to be fine, or so I thought.....

As we are all relaxing and talking I hear the now familiar hum of the little birds and see a couple feeding then taking flight.
Not an issue, right?

Soon enough we have seven humming birds shooting through the deck area in a game that is best described as tag. These little winged misfits start darting in and out of our group getting real close to my nieces husband. He is a big dude (he towers over me) and this tiny creature had him ducking and weaving like a trained boxer. Safe to say that some internet research was required to understand these little darlings better before someone loses an eye.

The deck would remain our peaceful retreat for the rest of the summer, although I did contemplate handing out safety glasses.

Now back to the adorable little blue tailed lizards.

We watched them scurry and play so often we started to name these cute little creatures. We had Elton, Katy Perry, Crock, Christina and Celine just to name a few. The boys would lay lettuce on the steps to feed them. It was adorable to say the least. The calm these little creatures can bring is spectacular (I was told if you have lizards on your property you most likely don't have snakes and I am onboard with that all day long).
This was a part of nature these little guys never got to see before so it was rewarding to see them experience it first hand.
Well, until they got to see the full circle of life play out, then not so much.
It was quite warm out so we were all inside enjoying the cool air and watching movies when life changed for us all.

 I kept seeing these tall birds run up to the house from the living room window. Now these birds are not cute little Cardinal birds,

these are like if a turkey and an emu had babies birds.
These were not one of natures beautiful creatures nor did they resemble the cute cartoon creature that was chased by a Coyote. This I learned was a Road Runner, very common to the area but ugly just the same. I let curiosity get the best of me and walked outside to see why they were running up to the house and running away.
Cows like movie night, would these critters find it interesting too? As I step onto the front porch, I see another bird come up to the house and peck on the wall.
How cute is that?
They are right up in our yard and right next to our house.
Nature is just full of inspiring beauty……or so I thought.
Upon closer inspection I see these visually unappealing creatures are actually pulling things off the house! Now our house is covered in stone so they aren't damaging anything like a wood pecker to wood but they are persistent. So I get closer to the birds to see what they are playing with.
I first notice they have large beaks but its when I realize a lifeless Katy Perry is dangling from said beak that I lose my shit!

These birds have been feasting on my lizards for god knows how long diminishing the population at record pace. I start running at these beasts screaming at them trying feverishly to save the rest of our lizards (I have no idea where Elton is and Crock is MIA). Not only do I lose the beautiful lizards but now it means I will have snakes in my yard (no idea if it's true but I am now declaring open season on Road Runners).
I not once heard the Lion King theme play in my head during this murderous spree so it is game on my feathered friend.

Time to get a Wylie Coyote and some TNT because those bitches are going down!

Well, I must have scared these birds because I have not seen a single one return. I was ready for them believe me.

School began and the boys were in heaven. It was their first year here and it seemed that making new friends came pretty easily. We drove them to school in the morning and picked them up at the end of the school day. Not sure how they would handle the long bus ride this seemed like a great alternative. Both boys were full of stories and updates on their day so every ride home was an adventure. The routine was working out and we had a couple happy little guys on our hands (big win I assure you).

Summer turned into fall and the holidays were creeping up on us, and that meant Christmas cookies or as I call it oven weekend.

Boys were eating breakfast so I figured it was time to fire up the oven. Cookies aren't going to bake themselves (I really need to work on that). Long day or two of Holiday spirit spilling all over my kitchen (well most people call it flour, sugar blah, blah,blah). If I could only get the boys to wear swiffer socks and run around the kitchen..........maybe next year.
So we are baking full force and the smell is just this side of heaven. You may have guessed I really love to bake and you would be correct. I also only use baking stones for all my baking (something I may need to reconsider). I love the way they cook evenly and just make everything you bake turn out great.......but I've got to tell you a few hours in and I felt like Rocky Balboa in the

last round with Apollo Creed. Those things must weigh 400 pounds coming out of the oven for the 20th time.
Seriously, where the hell is that little squinty penguin guy with the shoulder rub and pep talk?
And where the heck are my oven mits? Seriously, I own like 20 and I keep grabbing a new one.....when this is over I will pay the boys for each one they find (get in some training for Easter right?).
When this wraps up and the final timer goes off I swear I am going to scream..."yo Bobby I did it!". There will be a " Calgon take me away moment" to follow up to this years Cookie Armageddon!

Pause for a life moment......

Thanksgiving morning, turkey dressed and in the oven, pies on the counter. Crockpots and warmers going, filling the house with amazing smells. Family preparing to fill up our house and feast until food comas set in.
I love the Holidays and cooking for family.
Since moving south the guest count has risen dramatically and I love it. I was in full Holiday splendor awaiting the guests to start arriving.

Then the phone rings....

Our daughter in law states her water has broken and they are headed to the hospital (they live 9 hours north of us).
My first response was "that is not funny, if you are messing with

me I will kick your ass". Katie of course laughs but assures me it's true in a calm voice.
Now I know she is messing with me, there is no way she would be this calm in this situation.
I laugh and tell her to stop it!
That's when I hear my son Philip say, "it's true mom, I should be at work now but we are driving to the hospital".
Oh god I just told my daughter in law who is in labor I was going to kick her ass and on Thanksgiving no less!
 I am evil and I deserve all the hell the south is inflicting on me (ok, not really but lord help me here).
I have family coming over and tons of food cooking. I am having a grandson at any time and I need to go north!
I continually text my son for updates as the morning turns to afternoon and still no baby. I know that little stinker is waiting on me to get there but his momma needs to speed this along. We decide to let Thanksgiving play out and then take off.
Once the family was fed the cleanup was done and we were headed north on Black Friday morning to meet our 3rd grandson.
Beau Robert was born just one day before his mommas birthday and he was perfect! The perfect blend of both his parents and as sweet as could be (he gets that from me I assure you).
Bob and I were over the moon and exhausted but so happy to have another grandson in this crazy brood. We spent a couple days cuddling and kissing on this handsome boy and helping out a little. It was time we left and let the new parents adapt to life with baby.
Heading back home was so hard after cuddling this new little man. I think I was put on this earth to be a Nana and nothing else.

Pause for life moments..........

The "Donor" has left his employment yet again (seems to be a pattern) ensuring his sons do not get child support.
Nice, then states...." I don't celebrate Christmas I recognize Yule".
How convenient that he made that switch days before Christmas. He shouldn't worry his "Viking" head. Our grandsons will have Christmas and Santa will visit.
The key is to not create expectations and you can't disappoint right?

We are blessed to be part of these boys lives and trust me when I say......they are so much better off surrounded by family and loads of love.
The mountains are a big bonus.
Our first Christmas in the south was pretty spectacular. We put up an eleven foot tree and the boys got to do the decorating. Family came for the Christmas feast. It was definatelty a Christmas for the books. The boys got to meet Santa and he was very good to them. He even brought his elves along for the ride. Life is good on the mountain y'all.

Christmas came and went and the New Year was fast approaching, it was time to clean up.
I was seriously unaware the volume of paper and boxes this holiday was going to thrust upon us.
You know the trash pick up or lack there of saga we face "off the grid" so today I decided to burn the burnables (not a word but stay with me).
I gathered all the boxes and paper and headed outside to start a

fire.
The burn ban was lifted (seriously,that's a thing). I filled the barrel (yup we have one) and decided to fire up the trash.
I am not new to this so it shouldn't be too hard. I mean I have lit a bonfire or two in my day and don't get me started on the "vootvoot's (Sheridan Pit alumns know what I am talking about here- milk jug, stick and open fire make for good times).
Back on track, anyway is wrapping paper fireproof these days or is it just me?
After some creative measures I was blessed with the mother of all Christmas debris burn barrel glow (woohoo go me).

Flash forward a good 10 minutes into my happy dance when something started to crackle (not like Kellogg cereal crackle but like oh crap did I accidentally throw in popcorn seeds crackle).
Of course I decided to investigate, I mean come on, what could happen right?
As I sneak up on the barrel of flames slightly peaking over the rim a shot goes off. Whatever had landed in the barrel was now shooting up and at me with lightening speed. I am not a sprinter by nature but I can tell you that fear can get these legs pumping like a body builder in the gym. Unfortunately my reaction time did not match the speed of the mystery fireball that landed between my glasses and my eyeball.

Long story short, eyelashes grow back right?

I mean if they were slightly scorched and may have melted together.

Note to self, nothing I light on fire is worth a second glance.....let that stuff BURN!

Update....eyelashes do grow back but this is a slow process. Upside, look at the money I am saving on my mascara, lemonade out of lemons kids.

More amazing Ozark adventures.......

I snapped a couple pictures of one of gods hideous creatures that decided to visit today (an armadillo)....gross right?

Let me provide that backstory (cause well, it's me and there is always more to the story living off the grid).

Last night was a horrible storm with tornado warnings and high winds (yeah, been there before-not a fan and yes I blame the tornado)! The weather radio went off alerting us of the bad weather and of course I am just a touch gun-shy (totally understandable, right?).
Well let's just say I sat up most of the night certain an elephant was squeezing my chest (I checked, before you ask it wasn't Bob). So this morning when the alarm went off to start getting breakfast ready and lunches packed, I was more than tired but these boys wait for no one.
Once Declan was fed and headed to school (Ryland home with strep) I decided to get the roast ready for supper (yeah I am domestic like that since the garbage man doesn't pick up and the food gods don't deliver....ahhhh the struggle is real people) anyway.....I noticed that the high winds relocated one of my

pillows from the vintage glider on the deck to the yard.
It was in plain sight a good distance from devil shrubs and the holler so I decided I could reclaim my pillow no issues.
Bob is constantly telling me, and I quote "get your damn shoes on" before I go outside. I decided that was a good plan but wanted to be quick, so I slipped on my Ugg slides (side note- I really love these shoes) and head to the yard to get the pillow.
As I reached the pillow I noticed movement to my right (not going to lie I almost peed a little) and it was one of gods less vicious creatures.
As I looked at this possum in armor he was digging holes in the yard. Now I am as graceful as a dancer (sarcasm with foot surgeries to back that up) but holes in the yard are setting devil traps for my fragile feet (so not cool).

As an adult woman I was empowered!

I knew this guy could be scared off pretty easy so I do the most mature thing I can muster, I take a deep breath and yell HIYAH (like a good Jackie Chan flick with confidence and force).
I waited, and this demon never flinched.
Maybe armadillos have poor hearing, maybe he was the armadillo bully and was too badass to run.
At any rate I gave it another shot and was rewarded with ....NOTHING (arrogant jerk).
So I do yet again the most mature thing I can think of and rear back and shoot the best field goal kick I can provide (NFL is safe for sure)!
Just as I make a connection the bastard takes off (Charlie Brown moment when Lucy pulls the ball) and runs to the tree line but

not before I notice my Ugg slide is racing him to the finish line. Son of a monkey my slide was flipping like a fish on dry land towards the Hollar!

A soggy sock and a retrieved Ugg later, I decided I will learn to sew.
If another pillow goes exploring, I will make a new one out of old pillow cases and mismatched socks.

Lesson learned.

Life in the Ozarks was beginning to soften to me.
I think I am finally getting into this thing and having the little guys around too…..

With our children being in their late 20's early 30's it's easy to forget the impact of a spontaneous curse word or two, well until your 6 year old autistic grandson gets mad.
I can tell you that the Christmas Story furnace rant has nothing on an angry Declan.
This child made me blush with his skillful and correct use of some pretty high level profanity when his ABC Mouse would not load on his iPad fast enough.
Even this far off the grid we can get internet but I have to tell you I can one finger chicken peck type faster than a page can load on this thing.
So when this angel face baby looks you dead in the eye and says "GD, Fucking ass!"
You stand up and take notice.
I mean Ryland had his adorable inappropriate moments when he

was just five or so (came home from school explaining how his friend kicked a little girl in the nuts and immediately corrected himself by saying " I mean bagina") but he had nothing on Declan when it came to vocabulary.

So now we were left with a choice, correct bad words or pay for higher speed internet.

Both were going to be painful and nearly impossible but we all need to choose our battles……..internet shopping it is (keep the boy happy and he won't have a need to verbally debase his iPad, right?).

Ahhh, The Ozark Snow Day…….

Apparently in the south "snow days" aren't really a thing. They have what they call snow days but it just means if the mountain roads are ice covered no one leaves their house.

And because this was in the forecast all milk and bread was completely absent from the store shelves a couple days prior.

It just never gets old watching the panic set in.

I was used to seeing this in Illinois where they closed down roads seasonally due to monstrous drifts and high winds, not frozen puddles that were liquid before noon.

So today (early February) we were blessed with a "snow day". The boys were completely excited they had no school for that extra day off…..

I however, was mortified!

It was chilly and wet out so playing outside was a no go for the extra day off.
The roads were icy so traveling could be hazardous since we live on a mountain.
Two rambunctious boys being held captive off the grid.
My self preservation mode kicked in, where are all the movies these boys love?
Every dvd case I open is empty???
Do I have enough snacks for them?
Board games, dear god where did we put all the board games?
Let's bake something, I can let them bake cookies and worry about the mess later.
Oh god, what if the ice takes out the Internet or worse yet the power?
I am starting to see where "off the grid" may have more challenges than that of the critter variety.
In full panic mode I check the wine inventory (don't judge, a girl needs to have her priorities in order in times of crisis) thankfully my work family (pre tornado- insert shout out to my JCWhitney family here) sent me to a dry county in the Ozarks with an inventory that puts any vineyard to shame, whew..... I am good!

By the time the sun came over the mountain the ice was gone and the Ozark snow day was looking up.
All the panic and chaos was gone and the boys were happily watching movies and pounding brownies like it was their job.
I think this laid back life may just be working out for these little guys (oh, and the moscato inventory was not harmed in the

process) life is good.

Jump ahead a few weeks.....

Now our oldest grandson seems to believe he has mad skills in all things (except successfully going up the stairs but I digress).
This child falls up the stairs at least twice a week. There are 11 stairs, I repeat 11 stairs that take you to the upper level of our house.
There are Xbox games, cable tv (ok satellite, we are off the grid) internet and a toy store level inventory in their bedroom upstairs. Both boys travel these stairs several times a day.
Ryland cannot master the art of NOT FALLING UP THE STAIRS. It has gotten to the point that you can hear him hit from anywhere in the house. No matter how many times you tell them not to run up or down the stairs, it still has the same result. Fortunately he never really gets hurt but the boys shins look like he plays soccer with elephants.
I tell you all that to bring you to the events of today (Saturday morning with nothing but cartoons and breakfast to entertain us).

As Ryland is making his way up the stairs, (you read that right, I said UP the stairs) I hear the now ever present thud followed by the ouch heard around the world.
Of course I go to the source of impact to confirm he is in fact ok (I know this routine better than I know the alphabet).
Ryland appears fine, mad and a little embarrassed but still ok.
I of course ask him if he is ok to which he confirms he is and then I make the cardinal sin of all sins and ask........."were you

running?"

This child looks me straight in the face with tears in his little eyes and says "no I wasn't running, the stairs hate me, this house hates me! The only place I don't get hurt is outside!"

My sympathetic response that only a loving Nana can give………. "give it time, the outside will get on board soon enough".

And I wonder why these boys have a quick snarky attitude…..of course I blame their mother!

Weeks pass and the stairs have called a moratorium on the poor boy, at least long enough to catch him off guard the next time he kisses the stairs.

Today started out to be a good day (trust me I am always waiting for the last shoe to drop).
 Let me start off with...I love my husband, he impresses me almost daily.
Don't get me wrong there are days I think of ways to seriously hurt him but those get washed away by the sweet stuff. (To Bob's friends he is a really cool badass and my comments above are purely recreational-man card safely intact).
So we decided to make a shopping run (mandatory as we have no stores here aside from Walmart) to Mountain Home to get new shoes for the boys (seriously these boys must run military obstacles at school because these shoe runs are coming often).

This is about a 50 minute drive for shoes but totally worth it.

We are about 20 minutes in and Bob says "Jeezus Christ, there is a red wasp in here" HERE being the operative word, as in small confined area in the truck with ME!

We all know my history with these demonic bastards so I start to freak a little (thinking Bob is messing with me I start to imagine getting even- not funny). Bob then opens the back window (so he legit isn't messing with me-it's actually in here) and I really get freaked.

What the hell its only February 19th, yes it's 72 but don't they have a hibernation period?

Can't they wait to torture me until spring?

I got like a few more weeks of winter, don't I?

Is the groundhog in on this?

Did they plot this crap out just to catch me off guard?

Bob being my hero (on most days) pulls the truck over, hands me his hat for protection and goes after the spawn of Satan with a pocket knife! I got all swoony (not a word but you get what I am saying) because he went all Crocodile Dundee to save me from the venom of this flying bastard (see what I mean, all plotting to make him miserable washed away).

He opens the back door of the truck and begins searching for this demon.

The flying menace disappeared, this is more than a little concerning.

Did he fly out the window?

Could I be that lucky?

Just when we think the evil bastard has left, the red devil comes sauntering out from behind the back seat, seriously like he was in a line at Disney!

Bob my hero takes his knife and stabs the bastard (seriously big

wasp not a small knife) and flings it out into the woods!
I now have the visions of Bob the hero in my head for the whole shopping trip, yup folks he is a keeper.
Now that I know the flying Red Devils are out I guess I will keep the husband torture scenarios at bay and of course keep my hero close. Because there is seriously not a day in my new life that isn't full of something nefarious trying to get me....

Weeks roll by and the weather continues to surprise us, warm for winter months so it's rain in place of snow.
I am ok with that, I did have more than my share of Illinois winters. I deserve some good old fashioned shorts weather. I mean, I have things to do, stuff to fix (ok Bob has stuff to fix) so this weather is just what we need........or so I thought.

Today started like any other day (if you have kept up on my Ozark adventures you are aware this isn't always a good thing). So pre tornado (the Illinois nightmare that started this whole journey) I purchased a bank repo Jeep Commander (pretty certain my awesome mini van was not going to like the "off the grid" roads once we made the move- I have mad intuition like that unless it comes to critters and the hollar then of course all good sense vacates me like bad Chinese food).
I knew it needed work but hey, Bob's got time right?
Well we pulled out the seats so I could clean them with my Black Friday carpet and upholstery cleaner (love me some Black Friday shopping treasures). I spent a couple days cleaning them and today did some serious scrubbing and shampooing on them while Bob did some engine work. I finished the last seat when Bob pulled the jeep up to where I was working and asked if I wanted

to take a test drive.
Pretty excited that he fixed it so quickly, so of course I jumped at the chance to take this jeep for a ride.

Side note, we got hit with a lot of rain so our mile long driveway just about washed out (Yankee definition: we have a creek running through our driveway).

In my excited stupor I opened the passenger door only to realize it had no seats (I know what you're thinking, I was just cleaning them how did I forget there are no seats in it?). So I look to the driver seat and see Bob was sitting on a bucket, makes sense I can do that. We watch all those hopped up vehicle mod shows and if they can do it with no issues I know I can (first of many mistakes I assure you).
I look around and find a square bucket with a lid full of saw dust, not heavy so I grab it and jump in (second mistake).
Of course Dyme has to go (have I mentioned he is spoiled, oh and third mistake).
So picture if you will my butt sitting on a bucket holding my spoiled puppy dog preparing for the maiden voyage down the treacherous drive.
As we take off I am stoked, this jeep is running great, the ride is really good considering I am riding a tidy cat bucket.
Bob looks at me and says "we need to open this up" which I SHOULD have taken as "hold your ass cause we are going off road"(my fourth mistake).
As he puts the pedal to the floor we hit a nice gap in the road causing the bucket under my ass to take flight.
Now I am holding the dog with one hand and the oh Jeezus

handle with the other so.....without a third hand to hold the bucket, of course the bucket is going to have other plans.
I was still seated on the bucket but as I landed my butt chose this very moment to adjust.
Yup, never in my life did I ever expect to say "Jeezus Christ the bucket just went up my azz!"

Y'all have no idea the thoughts that go through your head in moments like this.
Like how do you fill out the emergency room paperwork and not have it go down in ER history (like the cat that was stuck in our wall and the 911 call I had to make back in the day, now that is an OPD story shared over and over).
This is a moment in your life when you know your choices have consequences and you wonder if the risk is worth the reward (clearly not in the instance).
Lord have mercy people this is something that makes you wince just thinking about it but trust me when I say.......it is way worse than it sounds!
I felt like I road my 1981 Schwinn 10 speed for 10 miles down a logging trail.
The way that bucket violated my personal space in the blink of an eye (no pun intended in case you were thinking of a brown eye joke).
Pretty safe to say I will be demanding butt rubs for the next couple of days so Bob will NOT be in mechanic mode.
Lesson learned!

Pause for life moments.....

Donor has stopped all contact with his sons. No attempt to get updates on their well being. No questions on school or health. The boys haven't even mentioned him which is a relief and disappointment. I pray they aren't silently hurting but I am grateful they don't have to battle the negative comments or conversation that usually monopolizes the contact. The cycle is real and all I can do is hope we can break it for them.

Now that "Bucketgate" is behind me (again, no pun intended), it was on to less strenuous Ozark activity. The weekend again provided us with amazingly great temperatures. The boys could actually enjoy some outdoor living, life is good.

Spoke too soon...

Enter the high winds and toys floating all around the yard (see I just can't catch a break). I hate the high winds (they are intense and I am still gun shy if you follow me) but love the warmer weather. The boys are jumping on the trampoline which surprisingly hasn't landed on a vehicle yet (knocking on wood as I type this).
Declan notices his soccer ball has blown to the infamous hollar. This beautiful little boy gets out of the trampoline enclosure and walks to the top of the hillside (ha, more like edge of the Grand Canyon) and turns to me and says " go get it Nana".

Now these boys have my heart and I would walk through fire for them time and time again, but I know what hell awaits me in the hollar (long pause to review potential life altering scenarios).
I put on my big girl panties, take the little guys hand and say "let's

go get your ball buddy"(silently dying inside from all that awaits us).
As I start to walk down the side of the canyon Declan steps behind me, takes his hand back and starts to push me! Seriously, he takes his sweet angelic little face looks up at me and starts to push me forward while saying " get it Nana".

Oh hell no!
This is not my first rodeo folks and that hollar is the devils playground.
I reach down, grab his hand and WE make are way toward what I am certain is our demise.
When we reach the tree line I look at this sweet little boy and say......."grab the ball Declan".

I know what you're thinking, I sent this poor baby into the newest M Night Shyamalan movie and where is that whole walk through fire mentality?
Trust me, I thought long and hard about this and came to this decision only because he is a pretty tough kid, he can handle it.
Does this make me a bad Nana, maybe.
Do I get to avoid the curad dance, umm yup.
Don't panic, the little monkey has mad ninja skills (seriously this kid can move like the shadows and never gets hurt, I silently worship him because of this) he retrieved the ball with absolutely no issues.
If I was smarter I would have recorded it for research because I know me, and that hollar will meet again and I won't have this adorably resilient 6 year old to save me.

Rant/craving meltdown….

We have been living "off the grid" just about a year. I never realized how spoiled we were living in Illinois.
Do you know there are restaurants in Illinois that deliver their most delicious creations right to your door?
If you crave authentic Chinese food, 15 minutes and you are eating it on your couch in your underwear.
You want pizza, a giant Chicago dog or all heavenly things fried, it's at your door!
Don't get me wrong, I love to cook. I love to make food people enjoy eating…… but if there is a possibility to have someone else whip that up and hand it to me without blowing up the kitchen, I AM IN!
Do you know that there is no store or restaurant here in the south that has or knows what an Italian Beef Sandwich is?
Let alone bring it to your door.
Bob and I spent several hours and hundreds of miles looking for the grocery store tubs of Italian beef (just to hold us over until we can travel back to Illinois to visit family) I am needy like that, to no avail.
They sell gallon tubs of chittlins (whatever the hell that is) but when I ask the employees for Italian beef they just look at me like I crop dusted them after ingesting a dozen eggs!
The vacant stare they shared with me solidified the fact I was completely out of my element!
Don't even get me started on the absence of a Real PolancicTenderloin!
I can tell you the translation to a pork tenderloin is not the same in the south.

God I miss Illinois food!
Sure, I can Betty Crocker that stuff up, but why can't I just buy it already?
Portillos italian beef, Sammies real pizza and Polancic's tenderloin sandwich……..I miss you like I miss my 20's!

I tell you all that to share this……

Today my niece and her awesome family came to visit (they are from Illinois). With them was a cooler that contained 60 Polancic tenderloins, 10 pounds of Portillos Italian beef with the bread and a few other imports that were disparately missed.
Let me just say, I have never been in mixed company and shared the big "O" ……..after seeing all these gifts I needed a cigarette and a nap (I don't smoke)!
Thank god stretchy pants are in style, crisis averted y'all!

Pause for a life moment….

Bob and I spent an entire day with my brother John working on mom and dads bathroom. We were adding a more user friendly commode, new flooring, a beautiful new sink and vanity.
Our parents house is usually a hopping place with lots of visitors so the upgrade was needed.
Mom being mom was secretly excited but was full of snarky little bites the whole day (I will never tire of her snipes or banter, she keeps everyone entertained daily).
Apparently when I told my sister Vickie and her husband Eddie we were doing this as a surprise it was also code for, tell mom how nice her new vanity is before she knows she is getting one.

Lesson learned…..

So now mom is full blown snark, full of piss and vinegar the whole day (definitely not big on surprises).
This is the very same woman who craved carpet so badly she spray painted our living room floor!
So when I decide that the carpet in her bathroom had to go, I am the "pain in the ass".
Every hour she would look at my dad and say "that's it, they have been here (so many hours) no more, I don't need it", dad just smiled and shook his head.
Mom called me some colorful names (little bitch was my favorite) but I knew she was just being ornery, she does that well.
As the day went on I began to realize we had no facilities (taking longer than expected to get the plumbing up and running). Sure the men could just go water the weeds but this girl was starting to get cross eyed.
You should note at this point I gave birth three times which also equates to tiny bladder with no patience. I was beginning to crack the whip on these men to the point they kicked me out!
Luckily the toilet went in and water on before there was a need for a clean up in aisle 6 if you follow me (I was the first to make the maiden voyage on that porcelain beauty-selfish, maybe; necessary-absolutely).
So 11.5 hours later and mom and dad had a new improved bathroom, woohoo!
Fast forward to the next morning when mom called to praise her new and improved throne room.
All the snarky name calling was worth it to hear her pride come

through when talking about it.

Now for a little me time......

Today we decided we were going to finally prepare the Portillos Italian beef for dinner. I was like a 6 year old on Christmas morning. The smell of the bread in the oven, the distinct smell of the beef cooking on the stove. I couldn't wait to get this sandwich in my face! My pure joy at the aroma floating in the house was amazing. That was until a certain 8 year old came running down the stairs to announce "that smell is disgusting, I want a peanut butter sandwich instead".
What in the hell is wrong with this kid?
Does he not understand that the smells permeating this house are bordering on euphoric?
The flavors as they reach your tongue can evoke spontaneous and sometimes embarrassing noises.
This experience is best described as bordering on biblical!
And this child wanted peanut butter?
I have my work cut out for me with these children no doubt.

I tell you all that to share this.....

We were sitting at the dining room table eating our Italian beef goodness (or peanut butter if you're 8) when I see a hawk fly past the patio doors.
That in itself is a thing of beauty, but a hawk flying by carrying a snake is cause for full on panic.
Here in the south if you see snakes this close, you have snakes in your yard!

I hate snakes, all snakes and the venom slinging bastards of the south are high on my hate list!
It's March for gods sake, don't they hibernate?
What is with these creatures?
I should not have to worry about these things until May, right?
Time for more internet research ……

Sidetracked by the Ozark life…

The south starts to get busy early spring so we were preparing for a busy several months in this Ozark bit of heaven.
The tourist season was fast approaching which means our daughters work hours were going to rise like the southern temps (high and fast). With two little guys depending on us to be here when mom worked Bob and I decided we needed a quick trip north.
We have an absolutely gorgeous grandson waiting for Nana Papa snuggles so a trip 9 hours north was a must.

Of course we have 2 sons and their wives to see as well but I am a sucker for babies.
I was also craving a good old Sammies pizza, a Chicago Dog and a Bianchi's pizza so it's going to be a win, win!
I am totally not a foody by nature but being deprived of certain things for a year can really make you go all Survivor. I was ready to scramble to just get a taste of those Illinois staples.
We loaded up the truck, dropped the spoiled dog off at mom and dads and started our "vacation".

I need to start with this to help you understand the importance of this trip.

I have gotten car sick since as far back as I can remember (I know what you're thinking, "so you moved to the land of curves and mountains?"). My dad describes most of these roads as following a drunk snake and I have to say, that is spot on. There are so many positives to living here (ok, maybe that's a stretch and my positive/negative list is still really lopsided) but I had pizza to bootleg and a baby to cuddle. So I sucked it up and prepared for the 2 hours of hell (the stretch of road before you hit flat land). We were going to have a great little trip and we could see faces we haven't seen in months. I had some Ozark Oven baked goods for my old work family, our family and a plan.
We arrived in Illinois and my shopping list came out.
We struggle to find things we took for granted living in Illinois so it was imperative that we grab everything we needed in a short amount of time (I knew my Black Friday shopping skills would come in handy one day). By dinner time on day one I had a load in the truck that would impress the best hoarder.
This trip was really looking like a big win.
I got in many baby snuggles, enjoyed a spectacular Chicago Dog and spent time with both our sons and their wives.
I ordered half baked pizzas to freeze and bootleg back to the Ozarks, it was all worth the 2 hour road of hell.
By day 4 I was shopped out, bloated from all the food and ready to head back home.
We loaded the truck up and prepared to get an early start home but not before our son Philip unveiled his addition to our haul.

Philip acquired a red quad runner and it too was making it's way to the Ozarks (our 2 oldest grandsons have been saving all their money in a jar marked QUAD FUND so they can enjoy the outdoors more). You may want to save that tidbit of information for a future rant.

As we make our exit from our former state we notice the cab of the truck is louder than normal with wind noise (still gun shy if you follow me). Bob checks all the windows while driving making sure their all up but the noise still seems loud.

At this point Bob looks up and pulls back the sunroof cover to see the sun roof has come open.

Now this just doesn't open slightly, of course it is full on up. Waving at passing cars like it's a parade. Bob and I both reach up at the same time and grab the glass. We are holding onto it going 80 miles per hour in the early morning. The grip of a lifetime on that glass for 2 miles until we can pull off to a gas station.

At some point the frame gave way and fortunately for us never broke off.

So now we are in the southern tip of Illinois at a gas station trying to figure out how to drive 7 more hours with a freaking glass shark fin on top the truck.

I head inside the station and purchase the smallest most expensive roll of duct tape in hopes my own personal Macgyver can get us and the truck home.

As I reach the truck with the platinum duct tape it starts to rain. My hero takes charge and 20 minutes later we are on the road, the sunroof secure and we are not getting rained on.

Before you ask, yup- still worth it, I have 11 half baked pizzas frozen in a cooler (not all for me, I figured if I was bootlegging Ottawa's finest pizza it was go big then go home).

There were several other key purchases in tow but you know....

priorities.
We get home in time to be greeted by a couple happy boys who make us feel like we were gone for weeks.
It doesn't take them long to see the quad and begin the happy dance of epic proportions.
At this point we have become chopped liver but the smiles on their faces make it worth the ordeal.

I have told you all this to get to this……

The boys now needed a place to ride the quad, not a big deal we have plenty of room. So Bob decided to mow the back hillside of our property a.k.a the gateway to the hollar (haven't mowed it since we moved here).
Declan was seriously jonesin to get on the tractor so Bob decides I need to take him for a ride on the quad Uncle Bubba picked up at auction.
Now to understand the situation you have to realize Declan is the reincarnation of Evel Knievel and is a daredevil of the truest form.
As I fired up Old Red to take him on a little ride to distract him from Papa I swear to you his eyes glazed over.
The look he gave me when he climbed on should have been a warning but nope I just thought ……this would be fun.

To start this ride seemed to be uneventful, that is until Declan decides we need to go faster.
This quad is equipt with a "whiskey throttle" which apparently means when you lose control you don't instinctively give it gas (good to know).
WHAT IT DOESN'T DO, IS STOP DECLAN FROM PUSHING THE

THUMB THROTTLE OVER MY HAND!
As we are turning around to head back to the house Declan pushes the throttle all the way causing the quad to shoot forward.
In those few seconds I kept thinking "save the baby".
So in one motion I grab this 80 pounder and gracefully jump from the quad.
Once we vacate the quad it of course dies saving us and Old Red from any damages. Declan looks up at me and in that brief moment I think he is going to thank me for saving his life but what I hear is "that was so fun!".
Clearly a 6 year old has a different definition of fun than I do. I now have a new definition of whiskey throttle and it involves a tiny little glass that can be refilled over and over. Ahhhh .....
Lesson learned.

Pause for life moments.......

The donor that advised us he was going to disappear for a while decided to call again. These beautifully challenging boys are growing and healing daily and vulgar condescending phone calls are huge setbacks. That being said because we were not expecting any contact via cell phone or otherwise we were all unprepared for "the call".
Declan is autistic and has made amazing strides since making the move here. This child went from daily melt downs and being classified as non verbal to very rare melt downs and amazing communication.
Sometimes he needs stimulation in very active situations so a little YouTube on his moms cell phone can be a life saver.

Until a video call comes in while he is watching funny kid videos. So when the call came in it popped up causing Declan to ask "who are you?" (Pretty sad since it's only been a year) but when donor announces "it's daddy" everything gains perspective. Declan replies with "no it isn't" and donor replies with "yes it is, how are you?" Declan in all his innocence simply says "f you", hangs up the phone and continues on.

If you decide to become a parent regardless of the way you do it, your job is love and provide for your child or children. Parenting and marriage are hard, there is no cheat sheet or smooth sailing. You struggle, you cry, you love, you celebrate and you choose all those things because it is what each child deserves. Every child needs to know they are loved and people who love them fight for them, help them and choose them over anything else. It breaks my heart to know that this isn't always the case. We will continue to love these children and make them very aware that no matter what life throws at us, they will always come first.
Declan has not once mentioned the call and the donor has not called back.

Blissfully unaware…..

Today started better than any other day and for me that is nothing short of a miracle.
It was Friday and both boys woke up with no battle (this never happens).
I packed Declan's lunch, got breakfasts ready (note the plural in breakfasts-they never eat the same thing so my kitchen is like a restaurant-place your order and wait).

Both boys got dressed without any arguments, meltdowns or multiple wardrobe changes (again, never happens).
I started thinking I have them trained!
Months of struggle has finally paid off and it will be smooth sailing from here on out!
I need to play the lottery cause this chick is on a freakin roll!

The day went smooth, uneventful and the weather was beautiful.
I got a roast in the oven and the kitchen cleaned up. If this is the gateway to a perfect weekend sign me up!
2:00 rolled around which meant, time to make the trip to town and get in line at the school to pick up my handsome grandsons.

This day was going so well I didn't even care that the line looked longer than normal.
When it was finally my turn to grab the boys I made sure my pick up sign was at the ready and the boys were ushered to the truck and belted in.
As I put the truck in drive Ryland looks at me with a very serious expression and says, "well I guess I had a good day considering its Friday the 13th".
What the hell is he talking about?
No way is it the 13th, no flipping way!
I grab my phone and hit the power button and sure as shit it says FRIDAY APRIL 13TH!
Oh my god, how did I of all people not know something so important?
I am now in full freak out mode!
I drive cautiously home waiting for hell to break lose on me.
I see a black cat playing beside the road (are you kidding me?), I

hurry past just in case he decides to cross my path.
I get behind recycling truck and stay a safe distance just in case.
When I think I am home free the truck in front of me loses a small motor off the back and it bounces onto the road right in my path!
Not today!
I will not let this day swirl into the shitter!
I am bound and determined to keep this day moving in the spectacular direction it started in.
I swerve to the left and avoid multiple issues and make my way home.
I get to the gate and there are cows everywhere!
Not a new occurrence these critters run block often but there is a new crop of calves that just aren't neighbor friendly.
I take my time down the mile drive to reach home.
Ha, I made it and everyone is no worse for wear.
I notice Bob in the barn working on stuff so I herd the boys to the house.
I take note that the clouds have turned an ominous shade of grey and the winds have picked up.
The boys and I gather toys and secure them in the trampoline to avoid the hollar later.
As I gather my purse, Declan's backpack and the 3 water bottles Declan decides to make a break for it!
I run to dump my stuff on the porch only to miss the step up and fall flat on my face!
My stuff flies everywhere and I realize I not only hit my knee on the concrete but my bionic foot of hardware smokes the edge of the patio!
Dear God I am dying, there is no doubt in my mind I have blood pouring from every part of my body due to multiple compound

fractures!
I gracefully roll over to my back and look up to see Declan's face. He gets down until our noses are touching and asks "Nana, you ok?"
My only response was a very loud "uggggg!"
I take a moment to inspect my surroundings before checking my body for damage. I have 3 water bottles spilling into my leather Micheal Kores purse, I have a bruise forming on my knee and a knot forming on my foot!
Declan, still unhappy with my response asks again if I am ok.
I simply reply "no, I am dying".
He looks me right in the face and says "oh, ok-1,2 corn Dogs?".
Of course he is hungry and his timing is perfect.
A couple of ice packs, a few pillows and lots of Aleve later and I survived my first Friday the 13th of 2018.

Or so I thought……..

Those gray ominous clouds turned into full on tornado warnings and insane winds (I am beginning to take all these storms personal). The weather radio went off more times than I can count.
Living on the top of a mountain has so many advantages but during storms, not so much.
The lightening and winds howling are seriously amplified up here. The skies at night are only lit up by the stars unless the thunder gods want to throw in a light show.
At 9:00 we decided to get the kids to bed and get some sleep or spend the night watching the news channel following the storms. The news won over and we sat up following the storms (it's what I

do these days since surviving the tornado that sent me here). As the reporters are showing some damage footage a crack of lightening shoots past the bedroom windows followed by a sonic boom that sent me like a cat to the ceiling!
I survived a tornado and this had me clawing the popcorn off the ceiling like I was digging for diamonds!
The boys come running into our room crying like they just lost a limb.
I grabbed the boys holding them for dear life and gave Bob a look that must have told him inspect the entire house for the bomb that just went off and NOW!
Minutes passed, but it felt like hours as the boys slowly calmed down. We all climbed out of bed waiting for the all clear. Once Bob confirmed the house was still intact and nothing was on fire I took them into their moms room. I climbed into bed with the boys to comfort them. If my mom was here I would have climbed in bed with her!
Once the boys were settled and falling back to sleep I slipped back into my room and started ransacking the cabinets.
Why do I not have any good drugs in this house?
I even yelled at Bob for not having any prescriptions!
I was looking for anything that would knock me the hell out!
I settled on a bottle of Kava Kava which is natures Xanax.
Thankfully those little suckers worked and this girl got a few hours of sleep. Friday the 13th one me zero.
Ryland has since been instructed to keep all calendar observations and spooky folklore to himself because the odds are always stacked against me.

The weekend rolled by and life went on. Thankfully the storms that rolled through took pity on me and left no damage.

Monday morning I woke up to the alarm and started to get my grandsons ready for school. Packed lunches, made breakfast and verified contents of backpacks. Their mom got up and readied them for the drive to school. Once they were off I decided I needed to get in the shower and get ready to face the day. I stepped on the scale purely out of boredom (unless forced I never step on a scale). I lost 22 pounds since moving "off the grid", I guess the food delivery gods were not my friend after all. With swimsuit weather approaching I decided it was time to take extra time in the shower getting myself more prepared for the warmer dress code (follow me here it gets good).
As I finish with my summer prep primping I hear my phone ringing.
This could be really serious so I definitely needed to grab it.
I fling open the shower curtain and begin to run across the bedroom to get to the emergency call.
I was stopped dead in my tracks by what is best described as clapping...
I immediately looked around expecting to see my husband laughing at me (he is a comedian and this would be right up his alley) but I was alone!
The phone was still ringing so I answered it forgetting all about the applause.
Turns out the call was just my daughter letting me know the school called and Ryland forgot his lunch in the van so she was headed back in to town to drop it off.
Crisis averted!
I hung up the phone and headed for the bathroom to dry off, it

was at this moment I realized.....
Giving birth to 3 children and embracing the kangaroo pouch all these years had not prepared me for the aging and gravity that my body was now enduring.
I was not be applauded for my Olympic sprint to the phone it was my body betraying me with a flesh flapping, half court, 3 point at the buzzer, game winning shot applause!
I could take this hard and really be depressed or learn a valuable lesson.
Lesson it is..........
I have voicemail on my phone so the next call I get while dripping wet will have to wait for my casual stroll to the phone, I don't need applause to embrace my greatness.

Now that I have that behind me I can get to the kitchen and start attempting Moscato jelly. I am in the south so of course I should learn to can things right?
What better start than with my favorite wine, that would make it socially acceptable to ingest before 8am, correct?
Glad you agree.

Life happens and sometimes catches us off guard.
 So when a frantic call comes in that your mom is headed to the hospital you grab your purse and run. Fortunately mom was going to be fine but I think I need to start shopping for a hair color. There is a crop of gray that seems to multiply daily and I think I may need to wage a war on aging.

Things to work on during this retirement journey.

Prepare for an awwwww moment here.....

My husband is absolutely AMAZING I was up later than normal reading (sometimes I just can't stop). So when the alarm went off before 6am I climbed out of bed to get the boys ready for school. As with every morning Bob simply says "morning beautiful " melts my heart every time. I don't have it in me to point out his failing eyesite.
Casie (our daughter) works late so this gives her a little extra sleep before she has to take them to school. Once the boys were fed, dressed and lunches packed I decided to climb back into bed to catch a few more minutes of sleep.
The Terminex guy was scheduled early so a few minutes was all I could get. Bob tucked me in and told me to take a nap.
After almost 33 years of marriage I am still crushing on this guy. I woke up and saw that the clock read 10am.
I slept the morning away!
Bob handled Terminex, hung my bird feeders and was getting my Jeep ready to roll when I finally made it downstairs, God I love this man, I am one lucky woman.

Time for some retirement bonding .....

Friday evening was beautiful. Bob and I sat on the porch watching the boys play in the large yard. City life didn't afford them the opportunity to run and play or explore. Living "off the grid" gave them a safe haven of fun to be had. So as we are watching these little guys play in mud and run all over I see Ryland head to the trampoline. I thought to myself this was going to be an early night. These guys were running, playing and now jumping out any

energy they had in them.
Starting to get ahead of myself I know.
So I see Declan has decided playing in the dirt is way more fun so I continue to keep a close watch since this kid can bolt in the blink of an eye. As I am rocking away on the porch I see Declan sit down in the grass. Now we have bovine invaders often so the grass can be sketchy if you aren't careful. Declan seems to be building something which has me glowing with pride. This child has grown and accomplished so much in just a years time. I was definitely enjoying his creative mind as he played and sang.
For a brief moment he dips his head into the grass and I am thinking oh no I will be checking him for ticks later tonight but he is having fun.
I see him do it again and wonder what in the world is he doing.
I call him and he looks up at me and says "not today".
Ok, now he has peaked my curiosity and I walk out to where he is playing.
I smell something awful and realize there is a fresh cowpie somewhere close.
I get to Declan and ask him to come closer to the house and he again says "not today".
I grab his hand and we walk to the porch.
I rub his head as I ask what he was building and realize my hand is covered in wet, green, smelly cow poop!
He was dipping his head in fresh cow poop!
Not once but twice!
Oh my lord!
Now I have to get him to not only come inside but to get into the tub ASAP to remove natures aromatic hair gel that he decided he needed so desperately.

I am seriously learning a lot about this whole country life and raising small boys...lord help me!!

The Ozark summer hit fast this year, we went right to 90 degrees daily once we hit April. So, Bob and I decided on a little home remodel change before the boys start summer vacation. We picked up some cedar to cover an exterior door opening that made no sense. I mean who puts a 24" door in a laundry room to the outside?
It's not like you can carry your laundry outside to hang through that door.
Seriously it's like maybe an elf door.
And who hangs out laundry anyway, especially here?
The little critters that you are inviting into your home with this practice is insane.
Bob and I decided to create a garden wall in its place. Some 2x4's, plywood and drywall and boom, Bob worked his magic.
So as we are cutting and assembling the cedar today, guess who came to visit?
I don't want to spoil the surprise so let me just say we made a fast trip to town to get wasp spray, 4 big cans!
As Bob is assembling and screwing in the boards I was on Red Wasp watch (aka red spawn of satan).
Clearly I was in survival mode because I missed the one that stung Bob in the hip.
Blood draw needles have nothing on these bastards.
I was pretty glad the boys were in school because Declan would have learned a whole new vocabulary of expletives today.

Now I am on high alert, they got Bob!
Nothing gets Bob, I mean ever!
These bitches have upped their game, I am so screwed!
We continue on, Bob the trooper isn't even phased. A stun gun has less bite than these demons but he just carries on.
As he is working I see 3 more come out to play, aww hell no!
I start spraying wasp spray like a kid with silly string at a birthday party!
Now you would think I would have hit at least one but nope, they are still dive bombing us and mad as hell.
I, of course, keep running and spraying not even looking where Bob is.
You guessed it, I got him too. I sprayed Bob with wasp killer. He just tells me to warn him next time and keeps working.
At that point I surrendered my can and grabbed a broom.
At least now my mad softball skills could come in handy, right?
As I take my maiden swing I hit one, knocking it to the ground.
I drop the broom and run to stomp this beast to its demise. It took 3 stomps for it to stop moving, 3! I am not a small woman and this poltergeist wasn't giving up!
Of course I trash talked and left it's carcass as a warning to the rest of these assholes.
I wonder where I can rent a bee keepers suit by tomorrow so I can paint this wall?
They are like the mafia and I am on the hit list now.
God I hate all creatures, they are killing my HGTV vibe!
Stay tuned folks tomorrow is another day.

Pause for life moment……

Bringing children into your home once yours are all grown can be so rewarding. Those moments when they steal your heart. It is humbling knowing that you are part of their memories as they grow. Things they will look back on when they become adults and smile about. There are also times that challenge you, things that make you question your own sanity. Today happened to be one of those days.

I can tell you our children did some pretty memorable things that challenged my parenting skills but nothing prepared me for my Declan moment of the day.

I try to talk to these little guys about choices and consequences but I never thought I would need to tell Declan NOT TO STAPLE HIS FINGERS TOGETHER!

Apparently that is a thing……..thankfully I have previously added carpenter and nurse to my amazing skills.

I just never thought I would need to use them both at the same time. Rest assured he is perfectly fine but I however have a new respect for the antique staplers ability to perform.

This life we are living is continuing to remind me to expect the unexpected.

Especially when this happened….

Bob has a tendency to play little jokes every once in a while. As previously stated there are days I plot revenge due to his antics. So this morning when Ryland asked that I make him peanut butter toast (after stealing half of my slice of course) I decide to go into the kitchen to Betty Crocker some toast for the boy. Now Declan is our eating machine but he was playing quietly, which is a rarity, so I don't disturb him.

As I am assembling the breakfast goodness I hear Declan scream "Nana, where is my pussy?" I was frozen in place, mortified to say the least.

What in the heck is Bob teaching this child and what will my revenge entail?

When I remain silent, struck dumb from what just transpired Declan comes into the kitchen and again asks "where is my pussy".

Ok teaching moment (I mentally prepare myself) explain bad choices and words that he can not use no matter what. Time to Nana up and handle this quickly.

When I turn around to see him holding one of his thousand Thomas trains. He looks up and says " where is pussy".

Shame on you Mattel, Percy is too difficult to pronounce for the age group of these trains! You knew all along this would happen and yet NO WARNING LABEL!

Bob is safe from retaliation for now...... I am still disturbed but informed.

Percy will be located every morning and on display to avoid this scenario in the future....lesson learned.

Now that the Percy debacle was behind us we started to pack for a quick getaway. Bob and I had a wedding to attend in Missouri so an overnighter was in our future.

We packed our bags, loaded the truck and grabbed the dog. Oh, the dog is spoiled but he was not going to be part of this getaway. Little Dyme-Bag was getting a sleepover at "crazy grandmas and grandpas" house. He gets to be spoiled rotten and they get to spoil him, definite win.

It takes 4 days to get him to eat real dog food after his mini

vacations but what dog can say no to ham and cheeseburgers? Dyme gets all the ham and cheeseburgers his little 9 pound self can consume so of course he loves grandma and grandpa.
My sister Vickie and her husband Ed were filling in for the boys while Casie worked so everything was working out perfect……..

Or, did I break a mirror or something?

We take off double checking room confirmation, wedding card and clothes. Everything is going according to plan I even got to stop for lunch and devour a Jimmy Johns turkey sandwich on the way (this sandwich is just this side of intoxicating), we don't have them near us so this is a rare treat. The bread, of course, will help absorb the wine I plan to partake in when the sun goes down (sigh). Full stomach and just miles from our destination, we pull off to fill the truck with gas. It's then that we are aware that we have a flat tire! Completely flat, like roll off the rim flat! Please god let there be a spare under this truck! We did not plan for any delays so this could be problematic.
We have a spare and a jack, the gods of travel are shining upon us!
The tire swap goes pretty quick with this hero husband of mine. So we get back on the road, we have nuptials to witness.
We get to our hotel with enough time to clean up, pre game and get to the wedding (whew).
That sounded great until we unlocked the door to our room……….

We have stayed at this hotel a few times in the past, not 5 star but always clean and comfortable. Once the door closed behind us things took a turn.

The smell of the carpet was just a little questionable (God, I hope it was the carpet)! I noticed a few flies in the room enjoying the atmosphere, gross!
We made a quick trip to the store for air freshener, a few fly swatters and wine, must have wine.
We weren't staying in the room long and we had to get ready for the wedding so I didn't have time to complain and change rooms. As Bob is showering I start spraying the room like crazy (much like the wasp spray incident). With fabric refresher in one hand the swatter of death in the other I begin my 20 minute workout.
As I am spraying and swatting I notice the fly population has multiplied, I kill one and 4 more take flight. I start looking under furniture for dead bodies, praying I come up empty handed.
I decide at this point to set down the spray and pick up the moscato (fantastic decision if I do say so myself).
When Bob exits the shower he sees that I have amassed a significant number of victims (of both the fly and wine variety) and just shakes his head.
This is going to be a great wedding!
Primped and pretty we make our way out to the rural field for the much anticipated rustic wedding.
Bob's niece whom we love to bits is getting married!
The whole setting is just beautiful, set in an open country field with timbered alter and the distressed white décor.
A couple white tents setup to house tables and beverages and shield us from the very warm sun. In my urgency to escape the Bates Motel hotel of horrors we arrived a little early and see finishing touches being placed on the venue (not late after all- boom y'all).
Time to chill and take in the calming atmosphere.

As the other guests begin to arrive and I notice a few do the whole BYOB if you catch me (ah, to be young and carefree). Ok, only a little jealous I didn't bring my own supply of fermented goodness to the show.
It isn't long before vows are exchanged and the new Mr & Mrs Caswell take off for the traditional photo shoot of all things Mr and Mrs. The guests begin taking seats under the main tent at the large number of tables, claiming their spots for the evening. It's then that I realize there is a "cooling station" which is a tent filled to the brim with cool air and cold beverages of the over 21 variety (silently doing the happy dance here void of any music).
As I make my way into the welcome to all things vino tent, I see a full bar with bartender doling out alcohol goodness in the form of ……….OPEN BAR!
I swear to you I hear the angels singing as the tent flaps close behind me.
Even though I did pregame it during my fly eradication spree, I was ready for all things cocktailesk. The bartender was simply amazing, having drinks started before you even made it to the bar (ok, maybe it was easy for him since I became a frequent flyer). As the evening progressed, cake and food behind us.
The music began flowing, and the guests filling the dance floor getting their groove on, when I see father of the bride making the rounds.
My brother in law is a quiet giant of a man, so seeing him in this setting was surprising. When he made his way over to Bob and I he offered up a bowl with maraschino cherries in it.
Now there is not a soul on this planet who would not partake in those sweet little gems, I am no exception.
I see the couples around us popping them in so I take one and

quickly begin to chew.
The party foul of all party was now exploding in my mouth.
What I assumed was going to be a sugary burst of sweet goodness quickly took a turn.
This gentle giant of a man was distributing cherries that had been soaked for days in hot freaking lava!
I was chewing and ultimately swallowing what is best described as hells fire!
After berating both my husband (he chewed one first) and my brother in law I decided it best to stick to all things liquid!
Unless of course you forget that one, it's 100 degrees outside. Two, the alcohol is flowing freely into my mouth. Last but not least three, the presence of a his/hers Porto-potty as the only place to release all things fluid consumed.
It is pretty amazing the skills one can perfect in times of crisis under the influence of open bar syndrome.
I can assure you the porta potty hover method is seriously under rated! Thankfully my child bearing, tiny as a grape bladder had mercy on me and I only had to hover a couple times (you have no idea how hard that is until you live it).
As the festivities wound down well into the morning, we made our way to the hotel. We had a long drive in just a few short hours so sleep came fast (I am certain I have the open bar to thank for that).

Now that the wedding was behind us it was back to our dry county reality that is best described as home. Adulting is hard people the struggle is real.

Oh My Shit!!!

So I am sitting on the couch live chatting with AT&T about the Illinois 911 fees on my cell phone bill (I have only lived in Arkansas 15 months now) while Declan is swimming in the pool just outside the window. I am watching him while Bob is outside sitting nearby. As I am discussing the fees I decide to throw in concerns about my poor signal (1 or 2 bars) and the issue with dropped calls.
Now Geraldine is being very helpful but she passes me off to Mario in tech who after 45 minutes says there is spotty coverage in my area so not a lot he can do.
Since I have been a loyal customer (over 20 years) Mario hands me off to Laura who is with customer loyalty something yada, yada.
Now with each chat rep. I am told I wont have to repeat myself as they have the chat log they hand off.
Well after copy pasting my conversation with each rep. I clearly had to repeat myself. Each time I am assured it will be just a couple minutes.....so as I am waiting well into 20 minutes with the 3rd rep. I see Bob jump up, interesting.
Declan has vacated the pool and is standing in the yard plugging his ears.
I immediately think those Red Devil Bastards are back.
To my surprise (or not) Bob looks at me through the window and yells "go to the front door and bring a broom".
He must be impressed with my wasp killing Ninja skills.
I stand up and walk to the door and he yells "don't open it, you will let it in".
Now my curiosity is peaked of course. I look out the glass door and glance up. I do not see any flying Satan so I think the coast is

clear. I open the door and step out to help this wasp meet its maker (I was feeling pretty bad ass at this point).
I look around, still see nothing but Bob is lifting up things off the porch and has the pool skimmer handle ready to swat.
I am thinking, ok he knocked it down so this should be an easy kill.
I look at him with my what are you doing face and he says....."it went this way but I don't see it anywhere".
I ask him what he is looking for, maybe it is a bigger bee.
Bob looks me in the eye and says "there was a 6 foot snake that crawled up on the porch as Declan got out of the pool and I cant find it now".
Couple of things here.....
SNAKE, 6 FOOT LONG, AND I OPENED THE FREAKING FRONT DOOR!!!!
Now I am on the porch looking for a snake but only see a small lizard jump out (that's a good sign).
I figure this is best left to Bob as I have Laura on live chat at AT&T waiting on me (I know, great timing).
I cautiously enter the house in the event the freaking python slithered in while I jumped out.
No sign of the sneaky bastard so I hop back to my chat.
I see that Laura sent several messages waiting for my response so I explain the snake issue but I am back now.
Well Laura must have felt bad for me because I now have new sims cards coming as well as a $25 credit on my bill.
I think that may help when I LOSE MY SHIT because Bob still cant locate the Giant Python on the porch!!!!

OK its just a black snake (at least that's what I keep telling myself) but come on.

Just as I am calmed down I hear Declan screaming for me to come to the kitchen "Nana, I said freaking Nana! I see a lizard" I am full panic mode and run to the kitchen ready to save a baby only to see he is at the patio doors looking outside at a legit lizard OUTSIDE.....dear lord in heaven save me!

Now I am officially on high alert.

I ask Bob to throw some clarifier in the pool since we shocked it and there is no way in hell I am going outside now. He looks at me and says Arkansas is playing and you know it's all about SEC now since we have no pro teams here. So I figure I would put on my big girl panties and step outside, quickly toss the chemicals then come back inside. It is still pretty light out and I will just look before I step.
So as I am tip toeing towards the pool looking everywhere for the elusive Python Bob takes this very moment to knock on the window as loud as he can!
SON OF A MONKEY!
I think I jumped 7 feet in the air and my heart is now beating outside my flesh.
I have clarifier on my cheek and a trickle of pee on my thigh! Asshole!
This is that moment I start running those getting even scenarios through my head because at this moment he is no longer my hero!

Tomorrow is another day.....

So there is this thing going on right now called a heatwave.
It is better described as bonfire on the surface of the sun! I think it was 107 today which surpassed yesterday's 105.
We have been pretty good at keeping the boys inside in the air to keep them cool. They get to go into the pool daily but don't stay out very long unless they can convince Papa to play in the pool too.
 Papa needed to do some work in his shop so I was designated pool party adult today.
At noon I made my way outside to spend an hour or so on the surface of the sun.
I should mention at this point I was sporting my new bikini since we have no neighbors and the boys love me anyway (big mistake) but I sprayed myself with SPF50 so it shouldn't be too bad.
Another mistake I assure you as it appears SPF50 is code for stupid people have too much faith in all that is SPF.
After about an hour the boys went inside to play Minecraft so I thought I would float a little bit and enjoy the quiet.
Yet another mistake as I seemed to doze off while floating on the sun's surface wearing what I now equate to cooking oil.
I was jolted awake when Declan came running from the house with a gallon jug of goldfish crackers to share with Papa. I figured I better vacate the pool and check on Papa.
As I began drying off my barely there bikini bits I realized I was more than a little crisp. Bob thought it best to show me via garage tool mirror how bad this actually was. I am now sitting in the central air vowing to never leave the couch and burn all undergarments as it will be a while before they can touch my flesh. Everyone else is a lovely golden brown and I am currently

the color of a stop sign.
Is it wrong to pray for snow in June?

The dog days of summer….

The heat, our second summer in our new home, has proven to be beyond any description. I think I pray for it to get "hot as balls" now just so it cools off daily.
When you wake with the sun and it's already 87 degrees outside you need to find things to keep your mind off the dripping the sweat beads.
It's so bad you can't determine if it's the irritation of the local insect variety or your flesh tears crying for relief.
Going through the garage and making room for organized storage is one summer goal. We are still trying to get the boxes sorted from the move as we still have a bunch.
Now that the shop was built we could go through a few boxes a day to donate, sell or get rid of our extras. This was a good plan, we could stay busy while cleaning up and organizing (enjoying natures sauna but having access to chilled beverages-win,win right?)
I think we had just finished box 4 when I noticed the wind had picked up outside the shop.
Now you have to understand that any time the weather begins to shift and dark clouds start rolling in I immediately become the town crier. I am analyzing every cloud with tornado potential and go all momma bear in protecting my family.
At this point Bob and I decide we need to close the shop doors and head to the house. Getting out of the steel shop was a priority since the tools and parts are the last thing I want in my

personal space once the twister hits.
I head to the overhead door and I am completely focused on the clouds and wind when I hear Bob say " watch where you step" in his urgent but don't freak voice.
Now we all know that my feet are the last thing on my mind when bad weather is rolling in so my response was to quickly look down and get back to my weather spotting duties. What I didn't expect was to see about 100 specks of "sand" rolling quickly into the shop right by my feet. It took about 2 seconds to see that the "sand" was in fact a giant army of BABY FREAKING SPIDERS!

This giant herd of insects were marching right by my sandal covered feet.
Holy Hell!
Where do that many tiny spiders come from and oh my shit where is the mother?
Of course there was no way I was going to start stomping them. My foot could probably squash 12 or 15 at most but not before the survivors plot their attack!
I looked around for anything to spray them with that would rush their demise.
I see a black can with a spray nozzle within reach and grab it.
I start spraying these tiny militants like my life depended on it (forgetting all about the live version of twister going on outside- ok that may be stretching it). I see the creepy little guys scurry and head towards the refrigerator.
The refrigerator with MY WINE in it!
I need back up they aren't dying fast enough!
I look at my can and see I have been spraying carburetor cleaner all over the floor! Just about the time I reach for another can of

anything Bob shows up with the real deal all bug killer in the gallon jug form.
I start spraying and holding them off with a broom while Bob moves everything out of the way.
By the time we finish spraying EVERYWHERE 5 times (seriously my she shed is in there- I am not rooming with spiders no way no how) the clouds have rolled on by and the winds let up.
We saved the wine from a spider invasion and I avoided a full on twister melt down.
Yes, I did crack open a bottle and yes I did drain that sucker dry- don't judge……and it isn't even noon yet.

By mid day I had cleaned up the kitchen, took a quick potty break (did I mention I pushed out 3 kids and my bladder is the size of a pea?) when I hear Declan yell. I am of course behind a closed door deep in my own thoughts so I fail to hear exactly what he is yelling about.
Declan is our personal town crier. If there are cows, woodchucks, deer or armadillos in the yard anywhere that child will spot and instruct while yelling for us to acknowledge his spotting skills.

 I decide at this point I should focus and listen a little harder to decifer just what this child spotted this time. When I hear my little man yell "Papa there's a bear in the yard!" I think to myself "thats a big woodchuck". I hear Declan yell again but this time he says "Papa get your gun, there's a bear in the yard!" Bob in turn says "we dont have bears buddy, is it a cow?" Declan replies "it's a bear in the yard Papa". I am up from my short break, wiping pulling up my shorts and washing my hands like the place is on fire! I hear Bob yell as I grab the bathroom door knob "holy shit

there is a bear in the yard!".
What the hell is happening? I run to the front door where the rest of the family has migrated to and oh my shit......there is a legit freaking bear in my yard! Not on the hill or in the pasture but in my freaking yard! This thing is wandering around sniffing and looking like he wants to taste my flesh and pick his teeth with my femur! Everyone is on the front porch watching this beast and I think am I the only one who is freaking out!
What is wrong with this family?
I have seen the Alaska documentaries, they find hiker remains in bear poop! They eat people, unsuspecting athletic people. The kind that run 5k's for fun and hit the gym after! I start thinking of the animal planet and the bears that break into houses for food! We put adorable paddle door handles on our house that have scrolly things making this an easy open smorgasbourd for the black beast! Why didnt I think of this when door knob shopping? Oh god I am going to be found in the morning scattered all over the yard and my bits will be mixed with bear poop!
Again, its just me that is freaked the hell out!
What do I do?
I call my mom! She is calm as I explain my situation and advises me to call my brother John(he works for fish and game) and they will come out and capture it. I immediately hang up and call my brother, he has lived down here 30 years, he knows what to do and he will save me from becoming bear kibble!
John answers his phone on the 2nd ring and I am relieved I don't get voicemail. I explain that there is a giant bear in my yard and I need help. John is the calmest person I know and at this point it pisses me off! Doesn't he know bears eat people? Specifically me?

John simply says (from my blurry pictures because I was shaking) its just a cub, he is just passing through. When cubs get about 2 their mothers have new cubs and boot the older ones out to protect the new babies so he is just looking for a new home. John assures me that since I dont have dogs outside the bear will move on and won't stick around. John also assures me that black bears are not aggressive and grizzley bears are the aggressive bears.
How long is this move on scenario?
How long does it take to break into my house and slaughter me? John tells me if it sticks around call him back and he will come out.
Can my phone dial from the digestive tract of a black bear?
Will my fingers still be able to punch in the number?
The bear goes across the yard and disappears into the hollar (that hollar is the scariest place on earth I guess it is fitting that the gigantic killer resides in there).

I end the call with John and decide I need to sit by the window and watch for the return of this monster.

Bob clearly sees that I am a mess and comes to me with the largest, coldest glass of amaretto to help calm my nerves. When that glass is drained I am presented with a 2nd glass (he gets me, he really gets me).

Oh, and the bear didnt return. I think the hollar got him, been there and can't say I am surprised.
Days pass and still no bear (thank god). Bob visits the Doctor for a check up, life goes on, right?
Well, I have to run to the pharmacy to pick up a prescription

where my sister Pam works. While I am getting the medicine Pam says "have you seen the bear yet?" In my mind I am thinking "oh crap she knows something I don't" the pharmacy can be the hot spot for local information, what did I miss? I start to panic thinking the bear was spotted again and he is coming back! Pam decides at this point to talk me off the ledge and starts to laugh drawing the attention of the Pharmacist (wonderful). Now the Pharmacist, whom I have never met, gets involved and finds all this very funny. It seems no one has seen Wild Alaska or any Discovery/ National Geographic shows on these monsters.....they eat people!!!! I advise the now small group enjoyng my hysterical meltdown that this city girl will be having none of this and grab my drugs and leave.

I decide to head to my mom and dads for a visit and also tell on Pam (I am the baby girl afterall). As I am explaining all this to my loving/ caring parents my dad looks at mom and says "did you tell her?" Oh my shit! Did they see a bear too? My dad loaned me his gun so what do they have to protect themselves? I start to freak a little and look at my mom not sure if I should be freaking out or not. Only mom is not looking concerned, she is full on belly laughing with tears rolling down her cheeks! Are you kidding me? This is beyond serious and she is just out of control laughing! Dad assures me there was no bear visit for them and that they are fine. My mom grabs her phone and calls my brother John and lets him know Bob and I are visiting (odd, yes).

Twenty minutes go by and John pulls up and comes in carrying a box (great!). John looks at me with his serious Fish and Game Officer face and says "I have your bear problem all fixed for you" and he hands me the box. I open the box half expecting a bear trap or something to repell the beast.

To my complete horror the box does not contain life saving bear repellant but contains one 48" bear rug (fake of course because my bear was the size of godzilla). I look up and John is grinning as he immediately points at my mom. John states "she guilted me into this, I wanted no part of it". I look at my dad who is pointing at my mom. Mom can't even speak she is laughing so hard! My husband is now laughing!
Lord help me!

Each day is the adventure of a lifetime......or is the adventure draining my life a little more each day?

As days pass we draw closer to the start of the new school year. The boys have really adapted to this new life and are officially starting their 2nd school year here in the south.
Shopping trips for clothes and final fun days are a must before the first day of school. So of course the remaining summer days are busy.
Backpacks are prepped and supplies all packed these babies are ready.

Bring on the day!

When am I going to learn?
As the first week of school rolls by the mornings run smooth. Until Wednsday morning when I get up to the alarm and enter the hall to head downstairs.
As I step into the hall Ryland greats me dripping wet with a towel

around his waist. Ryland looks up at me and says "we have a problem". Now he has peeked my interest. I ask Ryland what might the issue be? He looks at me and says in the most serious voice "I have diarrhea! I have proof, follow me".
There is not one moment in my life that I would have ever thought I would be part of this conversation.
Ryland walks into his bathroom, picks up his underwear and says "look at this, I thought I had to fart and water came out!"
Now I can confirm this child has had issues before in his 9 years of life so why this is such a huge issue has me stumped.
Ryland stands in front of me holding his underwear and says "I sharted in my Reebok underwear!" "Look at them, what do we do now, I sharted?"

I do all their laundry so I am confused why he is so animated over this but I continue on.

Even though the immature me is practically busting with laughter inside, there is no way I am letting this child see me break.
I tell Ryland we put them in the laundry shute and I will wash them today. I advised him to get dressed and we will go downstairs and discuss it.
This seems to pacify him and I head down to pack lunches and start breakfasts.
Ryland enters the kitchen and says to me "I need a note!" This makes sense he isn't running a fever, doesn't feel sick so he should be fine to go to school. I advise Ryland I will write a note to his teacher letting her know that he may need extra bathroom time. This seems to calm him and he eats breakfast without incident.

As I sit down and begin to write the special note Ryland stands up and says "what are you saying? Don't write diarrhea, can you write something else?" I assure Ryland that by simply writing issue instead of diarrhea the teacher will understand.

The boys leave for school and the day goes on without issue.

I am so out of practice with this whole small children 24/7 thing but I would not change a thing.

Well, by dinner time I was informed by my grandsons they were not eating anything off the grill. So the kitchen diner once again created multiple meals to satisfy the crowd. Chicken breast for the adults, corn dogs and fruit loops for the minors (they are eating, I am happy).
So once everyone is fed and ready to relax I see I have some baking to do.
I love keeping fresh fruit on hand for the boys. Snacking on that is always better than cookies and if they slack on the fruit consumption I can usually bake something out of it, again it's a win win.
With 4 ripe bananas on the counter I know I have the makings of an amazing banana bread in the morning.

I wake up ready to meet the day and get my Betty Crocker on.
As I make my way down stairs I am feeling a little out of sorts. Nothing that will slow my day down but enough to peak my Web MD curiosity.
I decide to start on my bread and when it hits the oven I will start my doctorate in all things medical courtesy of the World Wide

Web.
As I am mashing and mixing I feel myself getting warmer.
Odd I know, it's not like those cooking shows where they run around like crazy and compete for the spotlight.
I am just all chill in my little Ozark kitchen getting my bake on (not like Mary Jane bake but like flour, sugar & egg bake).
I decide to just pop over to my medical supply stash and take my temp, I mean I think I am burning up.
To my surprise I am an almost perfect 98.4?
Strange……..

As I am putting my medical supply collection away (carefully because I know I will be in this again) I notice my face is red.
Ok, now why am I burning up and my face red? I did not touch, taste or smell any berries (I am allergic and always have been) so it isn't that. I start to feel the heat from my head roll on down and figure it's time for Google. As I am scrolling through some god awful potential diagnosis (the scariest being pregnant, but thankfully my one and only biblical partner is fixed so I scan right past that one).I decide to check myself in the mirror one more time just hoping I was seeing things (oddly enough that points to yet another diagnosis and if anything I am thorough).
My nose has become flame red, not like fall asleep in the sun red but like bozo the clown red! I get up close to the mirror and try to see better when I notice something horrifying.
Dear god, I see sprigs of chin hair! Not like cookie duster mustache hair women spend hours bleaching, waxing and plucking (You know the disturbing shade under your nose that if left unattended lipstick acts like neon post it arrows saying "hey look at me") but like random splatters of armpit hair! Why am I

growing a freaking beard?!?!?!?
When did this start and dear lord in heaven how do I stop it?
I jump back to Google and am mortified to find that my god awful ailment is actually what is best described as……..
MENOPAUSE!
I begin to count days and grab calendars. Oh my god! My Aunt Flo hasn't been here in a few months! How in gods name did I let this happen and why did I not realize this was happening?
At a fresh, vibrant 51 I have discovered that aging is a cruel bitch and I just landed on her shit list!
I have just experienced my very first hot flash and it is as welcome as my very first period!

It seems that since the tornado struck (on February 28th 2017) my new normal is a daily reminder that there absolutely NO NORMAL.

I battle daily with the hollar and the creatures it shoves at us (that includes those damn red wasps).

I have become very domestic, not by choice (maybe there will be food delivery via drone in my lifetime-a girl can dream, can't she).

I have learned to find humor in our daily lives (that now include the antics of two little boys).

Menopause isn't a funny meme on Facebook, that shit is haunting!

Last but not least…..retirement will never be what you plan but it

will always be worth the ride.
Life is good y'all even when it isn't.

Stay tuned for my next book.......

Menopause in the Mountains
(a survival guide or documentary of my new hell)

Made in the USA
Lexington, KY
05 January 2019